Dora

thanks

Success Secrets 4 Students

for coming.

All the best

Marvin Munzu

Testimonials

"The session was fantastic and inspirational. I enjoyed the link between pain & pleasure and how they motivate us. Marvin is a very special man; it was very impressive"
James Springell (Pharmacy Manager at Denmarks's street pharmacy)

"The session was very interesting, lots of new ideas. I enjoyed learning new techniques to inspire positivity and also hearing how these techniques have worked for Marvin. It was interesting to hear his story/journey and the techniques he has used to get where he is."
Sarah Daulby (Commercial & Operations manager, Communitypharmacies)

"A fantastic workshop, a very interesting and motivated speaker, very interactive. It changed my mind set to be more positive. An excellent and awesome speaker"
Wen Chin (Pre reg Pharmacist)

"Good session, i enjoyed the tips to pass the exam and change of state of mind. It has helped me feel more confident i'll pass my exam. Good speaker"
Chloe Chong (Pre reg student)

"Fantastic workshop, i enjoyed it very much. i enjoyed how to get motivated and the energy throughout. The talk has boosted my confidence. yes! i will pass- state of mind. 10/10 as a speaker. He is doing a very good job, keep motivating"
Prama Yadav (Pre-reg Pharmacist)

"very entertaining, i enjoyed marvin's character and enthusiasm. It has help motivate me to study and to take up exercise! Gym time, also enhanced my confidence. 10/10, excellent speaker"
Edris Mahmud (Pre reg Pharmacist)

"It was an amazing workshop, i enjoyed telling my doubts to shut up. The workshop has made me more motivated to try the impossible. I give Marvin a 10/10, the BEST speaker i have heard"
Noor Jaffar (Student,Kings College London)

"The session was well put together. I enjoyed the interaction and the consistency throughout the session. It has highlighted the power of the mind on how we perform and enabled me to understand the mechanism behind changing our thoughts and actions. I rate marvin a 10/10 as a speaker"
Beverly Nketia (Medway School of Pharmacy)

The session was very good. I enjoyed how Marvin made me realise that i am in control of my future, all is in my hands and its not hard to change it. It has helped me get ready to take steps to change how i view myself in terms of working life. 10/10 for Marvin as a speaker"
Olivia Mbwadzuwo (UCL School of Pharmacy)

"I enjoyed the workshop it was very interactive, it made me recognise my current barriers. Marvin is a very engaging speaker, lots of energy and he really kept me focused."
Safiya Farah (Kingston University)

This talk helped me to re-analyse certain areas of my life where i have been limiting myself. Marvin is the best speaker. He motivated me to apply for a role i have been looking forward to.
Rachael Adeosun (Kingston University)

ACKNOWLEDGMENTS

There are so many people I would like to express my gratitude and appreciation for their support throughout my life and career. I would like to thank my wife for being my rock and constantly believing in me. I would like to thank my family, my parents for being my role models and my siblings.

This book could not be accomplished without the constant support of all my friends and work colleagues at Priory fields pharmacy.

Thanks to my career mentor Roy Christian who taught me how to believe in myself, develop my self-confidence and increase my employability, I'll be forever grateful.

Thanks to all my friends and my social media followers worldwide, I could not have done this without you.

Special thanks to Mitesh Shah from Mylocumchoice who has always believed in my vision and Elizabeth Chandler for suppporting me throughout my journey.

Dedicated to the special force within you. Your special gift and talent. Your ability to love and spread your passion and positivity to the world

Most of all for me, to Laila, Rania, Safya, Miranda, Tina, Julian, Jean Claude, Asu, Clara and my mum and dad

A percentage of all my book sales is donated to charity, thanks for contributing towards this project.

ABOUT THE AUTHOR

Marvin Munzu is a Media Pharmacist, a Superintendent pharmacist, pharmacy manager, fitness coach and inspirational speaker. Featured on several BBC shows, Marvin is the creator of the **"Success in Pharmacy"** programme. A programme which empowers pharmacy students, pharmacists and pharmacy staff with key skills and strategies to become outstanding and successful in their pharmacy career.

Marvin's workshops and seminars are attended by many students and pharmacists and are very **entertaining, inspiring and educating**. Marvin has inspired several students and pharmacists to become more confident, excel at interviews, succeed at exams, enjoy their jobs and achieve their goals

Marvin obtained a master's degree in pharmacy (Mpharm) from Kingston University (London) and a Bsc (Hons) in Pharmaceutical Management from Bradford University.

He is a media pharmacist and features regularly on the BBC Breakfast show, BBC Radio Cambridgeshire, BBC Look East TV, The Guardian newspaper and several other media. He has also written several press releases.

Marvin lives in Northamptonshire with his wife and two children

TABLE OF CONTENTS

CHAPTER 1

What you will learn in this book

This is the first motivational and inspirational book written specifically for students. It focuses entirely on you, the student. It is written by someone who deeply cares about your success and has been through most of the challenges you are going through.

Over the next few chapters, you will discover cutting edge strategies, techniques, skills and philosophies which helped me to succeed as a student, pharmacy manager, superintendent pharmacist, BBC featured pharmacist, inspirational speaker, personal trainer, UK natural bodybuilding champion, author and creator of the *"Success in Pharmacy"* programme.

My experiences in this book are from my life as a student and pharmacist. It also includes information from surveys from a range of students on their most common challenges faced at university. Throughout this book, you will discover unique and practical solutions to most of these challenges. You will uncover vital information which you don't learn at university or college but which is important for success at university and beyond.

The ideas, philosophies and strategies in this book are universal and can be applied by anyone in any walk of life.

MY PROMISE TO YOU

If you apply the strategies in this book, I promise you will be more confident, more energetic and passionate. You will feel in control of your goals, dreams and aspirations. You will manage your time more effectively, be extremely productive and efficient, and feel energised and revitalised.

You will excel at exams and be outstanding at job interviews. You will ignite your passion and be empowered to achieve and realise your true potential quicker than most other students. You will enjoy your course and become a leading and successful professional when you graduate.

I am writing this book as a companion on your journey. To help you overcome certain challenges which you will face now and in the future. As a guide, a mentor, a coach and a friend on your amazing student journey.

I used to ask myself several questions when I was at university. Questions such as; "how can I manage my time more effectively? How can I manage my time to cope successfully with the endless number of courseworks, tests, assignments, exams and deadlines?

How can I manage my money better? How do I ensure my outgoings are less than my incomings? How do I stay out of debt and simultaneously invest whilst studying?

How can I study efficiently so that I can retain and apply most of the knowledge that I learn in lectures and excel at exams and tests?

How can I balance my social, academic and work life to still spend quality time with my family and friends without my studies suffering?

How can I stay fit and healthy? What kinds of foods can I eat to feel energised and revitalised?

How can I prepare myself for life after university or college? How can I develop good interview skills, build my self-confidence and develop profound attributes which employers look for such as, decision making, communication, problem solving and teamwork skills?

What jobs should I apply for? How can I prepare myself for the competitive job market after my course?

I will reveal to you powerful solutions which helped me overcome most of these challenges.

The tools which I show you in this book are very unique and life changing and I am very excited to share them. I believe we have a lot in common and throughout this book I will act as a facilitator to help you achieve your desired outcomes and overall success.

Another reason I am writing this book is because when I was a student I wished I had a mentor. A professional I could relate to, someone who was dedicated to helping me succeed, someone who was able to teach me things and tell me things from their experience that I wasn't taught at university or college. A person who fully understood my challenges.

This book is my gift to you, an asset which I did not have in my student days. I am extremely grateful to be on this exciting journey of success with you and I promise you that by the time you finish reading this book, you will feel more confident in yourself and your abilities. You will feel empowered to take action and move in the positive direction you desire and deserve. You will feel motivated and focused.

MY Journey

In 2003, I graduated with a pharmaceutical management degree from the University of Bradford. I was very excited until I started applying for jobs. Every job I applied for I was rejected because I did not have the required skills and I was devastated. In one month I applied for 10 jobs and I got 10 rejections.

I lost my self-confidence. I had no family to support me as my family lived abroad. I was broke and I struggled to pay my rent. One morning there was a loud knock on my door, I jumped out of bed, with my heart racing, I ran to the door and opened it. In front of me was my landlord Mr Hussein. He had a long white beard, long white robe, was slim, tall and he was fuming. He yelled furiously "It's been 3 months since you paid your rents, I want you out of my house now" and he threw me out of his house.

I remember walking down the streets of Bradford, pulling my black suitcase with nowhere to go. I had no family in Bradford to go to. I called a friend who offered me a place on his sofa until I found a job. I stayed with him for just over a year.

During this time, I lost my self-confidence. I was so embarrassed of what and who I had become. I cut contact with most of my family and friends. When my family contacted me, I pretended everything was fine and I had a good job and life was great. I was too embarrassed to tell them the truth about my situation and I hid the truth from them.

I did very low paid jobs such as, stacking shelves, cleaning, working in warehouses and supermarkets to make ends meet. The most demoralising job was selling double glazed windows door to door. Every door I knocked got slammed in my face.

One afternoon I felt depressed, I sat down on my friend's sofa in his living room and began asking myself questions as tears dropped down my eyes. How did I end up here? Why is this happening to me? What have I done to deserve this? Why me? Why can't I get a good graduate job?

I started surfing the internet for positive articles to cheer me up and I came across an article by a motivational speaker called Tony Robbins. Tony said something in this article which radically changed my life.

Tony said *"for things to change in your life, **you** have to change"*

This made me realise that I was responsible for my circumstances and I had the power to change them. I began to change every single belief about myself. My thoughts, my capabilities, my abilities and my skills. As I began to change myself from within, I noticed that everything around me began to change positively.

I studied a science called Neuro Linguistic Programming (NLP). A fascinating science of achievement and peak performance. I applied NLP principles to improve myself and I produced incredible results.

NLP principles and techniques helped me to regain my confidence. It boosted my ability and unlocked my potential. I started becoming successful in all areas. I got my first graduate job with the NHS and I was one of the 7 successful candidates out of 350 applicants. I had turned things around and made a major breakthrough.

I was inspired to return to university and study pharmacy. Throughout my degree, I continued to apply these strategies and techniques. They helped me succeed at university. These skills and tools have brought me to where I am today and all the success I have achieved along the way.

Now my goal in life, my purpose and my mission is to share my stories and these NLP tools and techniques with as many students and professionals as possible, so that you don't have to go through the same challenges which I went through and you can benefit greatly from these skills in all areas of your life.

CHAPTER 2

MOTIVATION

Motivation is one of my favourite topics and over the years it has become a word many people associate me to. I once received a message from a pharmacist who asked me 'how do you work full time and still have time for motivation?"

I replied *'everything we do in life is connected to our level of motivation"*, either through motivating ourselves or others. Our motivation drives our actions and our actions produce results and shape our destiny.

The more motivated you are, the more actions you will take and the more results you will produce. I recently interviewed a group of students and I asked them what were some of their greatest challenges and all of them said, motivating themselves to meet deadlines and to study daily.

Learning how to motivate yourself instantly is one of the most important skills which will help you at university, college and throughout life.

Studying is about motivating ourselves to gain valuable knowledge and then applying this knowledge to producing results.

As a student you need to be able to motivate yourself to study, motivate yourself to stay fit and healthy, motivate yourself to do certain things you are not comfortable with to get the results you want.

When you become a graduate and start working, there'll be many challenges which require motivation. There'll be lots of things to learn, many clients and colleagues to motivate from time to time, many targets which you will need to achieve, many courses to attend and a lot of other demands in your personal life.

What controls our motivation?

Our motivation is controlled by two forces. *Pain and pleasure.* It sounds very simple but it is true. Human beings naturally move towards pleasure *and* away from pain.

For example, have you ever procrastinated? We all have. Why do we procrastinate? Can you remember a time when you put off completing an assignment until the deadline?

You knew you had a deadline but each time you thought of doing it, you linked it to pain. Maybe you felt it was too time consuming, or doing it would make you miss your favourite TV programme or that it looked too difficult and boring.

So you linked pain to *doing* the assignment and pleasure to *not doing* it. As time went on and the deadline approached you finally got yourself to do the coursework the night before the deadline. So what happened? What changed? What made you actually get up and finally do it?

The reason you did it was because you changed what you linked pain and pleasure to in your brain. At the beginning you focused on the pain of **doing** your assignment. But the night before, you changed your focus, you now started focusing on the pain of **not doing** your assignment. Maybe you would fail the entire module and potentially ruin your final result, so you got yourself to do it.

If you link a lot of pain to anything, you will avoid doing it and if you associate a lot of pleasure to anything you'll move towards it. The challenge is most of us let these associations happen **unconsciously** and thus we are not in control of what we link pain or pleasure to.

"The goal is to learn to use pain and pleasure rather than let pain and pleasure use you"

I remember when I began my first year at university, most of the students I hung out with loved partying every night. I found this very pleasurable and spent a lot of my time partying and I did not focus as much on my course. After a while my grades declined and I started focusing on the pain of partying and the negative consequences of spending so much time with these groups of friends.

I decided to spend less time with these friends and more time with new friends who were more focused on studying. I made this change because I changed what I linked pain and pleasure to.

In my 'Success in Pharmacy' workshops, I usually get all the participants to do an exercise at the end of the workshop, a motivational exercise where they write down some negative behaviours, habits or beliefs about themselves which they want to change. For example, a belief like 'I am not good enough'.

They write all the pain this belief has caused them in the past in all areas of their life, the pain it's causing now and the pain it will cause in the future if they don't change it now. They are able to visualise the past, present and future and link this negative belief to intense pain.

I also ask them to write down something or a positive belief about themselves or an action they'll like to adopt consistently for example; revising daily or eating healthily, or being more confident and then I ask them to write down all the benefits they'll get if they adopted this new belief of behaviour.

In each case, after doing this exercise and visualising, they all instantly feel more motivated to stop the negative behaviour or belief and very motivated to adopt the new one. It is an amazing exercise which produces instant results and a change in state

Now try the exercise and notice how motivated you feel at the end.

MOTIVATION EXERCISE

Write down a belief or behaviour you'll like to change.

Write down all the pain it has caused you in the past, present and what it will cause you in the future if you don't change it.

Past

Present

Future

Write down a new belief or behaviour you'll like to replace this with.

Write down all the benefits you'll get if you adopted this new belief/behaviour now and in the future.

Today

Month

Year

FINDING YOUR INTERNAL DRIVE

We are all motivated by different things. We all have different values and different things that drive us. For example, some students could be motivated by different professions and different work environments

Our motives to act are all different and we all have a hierarchy of needs. Certain things mean more to us than others and we make our decisions based on our value system.

To motivate yourself and others around you, it's important you understand what drives you and each individual you are trying to motivate. You need to understand their needs.

I remember a good friend of mine whose main motivation was money. He wanted to earn more money but was not keen on studying any new courses or attending educational seminars. I tried to persuade him several times to attend some personal development seminars with me but he wouldn't.

When I realised he was mainly driven by money, I had to figure out a way to connect money directly to one of the seminars. I invited him to one seminar which spoke about how you could make more money by completing this one year course. If he completed the course, he would earn twice as much. My friend was very excited about attending this seminar. He was so driven and enrolled on the course and within a year was earning twice his income.

The reason I failed the previous times to get him to attend the seminars was because I was focusing on the benefits of the seminar from my point of view rather than his. But the moment I was able to associate it with something he truly valued, he became motivated instantly. Understanding what motivates us and what motivates the people around us is vital if we want to influence them.

There are 6 forces that drive us, 6 basic needs.

1) Certainty

We all have a need for certainty. We need to be sure that what we are doing will guarantee pleasure and avoid pain. For example, my friend wanted to be guaranteed he would earn more money at the end of the course. One of the reasons most of us choose to study pharmacy is because of the guarantee of job security after graduation or the guarantee of earning within a certain salary range. It is true there are no guarantees in life but the certain professions have higher prospects than others

I once received a message from a student who was in his second year of pharmacy and was asking my advice on whether to quit the course and study either medicine or dentistry which he thought were more certain. In light of the recent proposed pharmacy cuts, he had received a lot of negativity from pharmacists about the uncertainty of pharmacy. He needed to be certain pharmacy was the right choice for him and would guarantee him pleasure and not pain.

I know several cases of friends who have left pharmacy after practising for several years because of the uncertainty. We are all driven by a desire for certainty.

One of the greatest forces which drive us is our need for certainty, certainty we will graduate, certainty we will get jobs after graduating, certainty we have what it takes to pass the degree and become successful after university or college.

2) Uncertainty

This sounds contradictory but although we all have a need to be certain that we will have jobs after university, that we will pass our exams, we also have a fundamental need for uncertainty or variety.

When we have a lot of certainty we become bored. We thrive and get motivated by variety. How many times have you sat in a boring lecture because it was very monotone with no variety?

Or have you ever been in a relationship and found it to be very boring because it was so predictable? There was no variety, no surprises, nothing new and you were bored out of your mind?

One of the most common patterns with recent graduates, is straight after graduating they are filled with so much energy, drive and ambition. They are motivated by the change, the variety, being the a professional, earning money and a change in status.

But something happens a few years later. Most of these graduates start losing their drive and motivation. They start getting bored of routine tasks and habits and eventually start looking for new challenges, new jobs, new roles or new ways to add some variety or uncertainty to their jobs.

3) Significance

We all have a desire to be different, to stand out, to be unique. This is what gives us the edge at job interviews. We highlight what's different about us from other candidates. Having a degree does not make you different from other graduates, your personal skills do.

Significance differentiates you from the competition. Many students feel significant in different ways. For some students you may be the 'coolest' in the class, maybe the most intelligent student or the best dressed, the most flamboyant, the most popular or the most confident.

Sometimes just having a title or being part of a group could make you feel significant, for example a society president, a team captain or an award winner. The need to be significant and differentiate ourselves from everybody else is a great motivator.

4) Connection

We also want the opposite of being different. Sometimes we want to connect and be treated like everyone else. We want to be part of a group or a society. How many times have you heard people say 'I just want to be treated like everybody else'? We want to be different but at the same time we are driven by a desire for belonging. Being part of a team, part of a group or a social network.

For example; it is amazing when most students attend student annual conferences. The feedback, messages and pictures all over social media are incredible. There is a deep sense of connection and belonging. Many students write comments about these events being the best event of their lives, or meeting the best and most inspiring people.

We are motivated by connection, we want to be part of a group, part of a team, part of a society. To be part of a society or association.

5) <u>Growth</u>

We all need to grow. When we do not grow we lose our drive. We get excited when we progress from the 1st year to the 2nd year, 3rd year to graduation. This transition and progress motivates us. If we do not grow in all areas of our lives, our relationships, our career, our family, spirituality and finances, we become discontent.

One of the ways we become depressed is if we feel our circumstances are worse today than they were yesterday. The opposite is also true. We get motivated when we look back and our circumstances are better today than they were yesterday. The mere transition from a student, to a graduate trainee is a great motivational boost as your knowledge, responsibility, finances, status and influence all increase.

Our college or degree programmes are motivating because we grow in knowledge over these years. The same applies when you graduate and many graduates look for various opportunities to grow in different ways. There is a sense of joy and gratification when we feel we have gained and have become more today than we were yesterday.

The more we grow, the more valuable we become in all aspects and the more we can make a difference and impact to the lives of the people around us.

Every day you must ask yourself certain questions. What can I do to keep growing in all areas of my life? How can I make more money? How can I achieve better grades? What new knowledge or skills can I learn today that will have a positive influence on my life or career tomorrow?

What spiritual books or knowledge can I learn? What new activities can I do that will grow my relationships and improve my health and wellbeing?

By constantly focusing on new ways to grow, you will continuously be filled with abundant energy and motivation.

6) Contribution

The final need is a desire to give back, to contribute, to make a difference. Most of us will do more for people we truly love than for ourselves, for example our parents, children or loved ones.

We want to make a difference in some way and add value. For example, many students are involved in charity events which gives them a sense of contribution. Or we buy our loved ones special gifts. Sometimes we may contribute in little ways such as; helping a friend move house, or teaching a colleague a subject you understand which they find difficult, or just inviting them for a meal.

Contribution can also be through words, for example; words of encouragement, words of support, some positive advice or action to improve someone's life.

Contributing gives us a sense of worth and meets our higher spiritual need. I have always believed *"giving is the key to living"*. We are designed to add value and to contribute and the more you give your time, your energy and support to others, the more you shall receive.

The need to grow and contribute, to help and support others is what makes life meaningful and fulfilling. Success without fulfilment is the ultimate failure.

For this reason, a percentage of all my book sales are donated to charity to help educate and improve the quality of valuable lives. By purchasing this book, you are contributing and supporting many less fortunate lives. You are enhancing and creating opportunities for many to succeed.

EXERCISE

Write down different ways in which you can contribute. What can you do today for someone you care about? What can you give back to society? What charity can you support? Who can you help by giving advice or words of encouragement? What can you do today to improve someone's life?

CHAPTER 3

Turning your student goals into reality

Being able to set empowering goals is one of the most important and rewarding skills you can develop at university and throughout your life. Goals drive us, we are designed to move towards achieving our goals.

Being able to set clear goals in all areas of your life gives you great focus, drive and direction. One of the quickest ways to achieve so much in little time is to master the art of goal setting.

Whatever you want to achieve at university whether it is a first class degree, to manage your money more effectively, improve your health and wellbeing, you can achieve it by learning a few basics about goal setting.

Follow these few tips on goal setting and you'll be more focused, more motivated and you will achieve so much in a short space of time. These are the steps to turn your goals into reality.

1) **Define your goals clearly**

   Clarity is power. The clearer you define your goals the more energy you will have to achieve them. Be specific. The challenge for most of us is we are not very specific or clear on exactly what we want to achieve, hence we lack the drive and momentum to achieve what we want.

   For example, most of us set New Year resolutions but hardly achieve them because they are not clear enough. To make a goal more specific you need to ask yourself several questions such as; when do you want it? Why do you want it? What type of person do you need to become to achieve it? Who can help you achieve it? What resources do you already have to achieve it?

Rather than just say 'I want to lose weight' which is very vague and ineffective, you can add more clarity and specificity by saying 'I want to lose 6kgs in 6 months by exercising daily for 1 hour in the gym with my personal trainer and eat mainly fruits, vegetables, complex carbohydrates and white meat. I will know I have achieved my goal when I am able to fit easily into my size 8 Calvin Klein jeans.

This is a more empowering goal as it is more specific than 'I want to lose weight'. Being more specific makes the goal more achievable and enhances your drive and desire to achieve it. Our subconscious mind is always working towards a direction and if you don't direct your mind consciously, someone will.

Setting goals makes you focus on what you want. Most of us don't achieve our goals because we focus on what we don't want rather than on what we want. If you keep focusing on what you don't want, you will get more of it. For example, if I say to you 'don't think of the colour blue' did you think of blue? Yes, or no? Yes, you did, because when you focus on what you don't want you get more of it.

In my seminars, I usually ask the students, 'what do you want in life?' and a few tell me 'what they don't want' instead.

If you want to become a very successful student, then the first thing you must develop is a clarity of vision. You must know clearly and specifically what you want to achieve, what you want in life. Your ability to define what you want and what others want is one of the key skills to personal and professional success.

So let's show you how to define your student goals clearly, so that you become more empowered and driven to achieve them.

There are a few key steps you must follow to set effective goals.

1) State all your goals in the **positive** tense. Focus on what you want and not on what you don't want.

2) Be clear and specific:

Clarity is power and the clearer you are, the higher your chances of achieving your goal. The way to get clear is to ask yourself several open questions when setting your goals. What, when, who, why questions. When will you achieve the goal? Who with? Why is this important to you? How will you achieve it? What will you do?

You need to ensure that your goal is measurable. It should be sensory based, the more sensory based it is, the higher your chances of achieving it. For example, what will you see when you achieve your goal? What will you hear? How will you feel? Engage all your senses, they will empower you.

If you do not know your evidence, then you may achieve your goal without knowing you have achieved it and still be unfulfilled.

Finally, you must take control. The more control you have over your goal, the more flexibility and momentum you get. If your goal depends on other people, then you will have less control and will become frustrated and you will give up or blame others for failing to achieve them. Set goals which do not rely greatly on other people but on you.

It is also imperative that your goals fit in with your core values. If you set goals which do not align with your values, then you will not be driven to achieve them and you will self-sabotage.

For instance, if one of your key values is to spend so much time daily with your family and friends, then setting a goal to get a high profile international job which requires flying around the world constantly to attend meetings will not be ideal for you.

How to Turn your goals into reality

1) Dream

What do you want? Write down all the things you want to achieve at university and after university. The key is to have no limit in your imagination, let your imagination run wild, do not think about how you will achieve them and do not place any limitations at this stage. Imagine everything was possible, what would you do?

The best way to do it is to think "what will you do if you knew you could not fail? What will you want to achieve? What sort of things will you want if you knew you could not fail?

Put yourself in this frame of mind, let your imagination run wild, and write down all the things you'll do and all the goals and things you'll want if you knew you could achieve anything?

2) Time frame

Now go over the long list you have made and assign each of the goals a deadline. Give each goal a time frame in days, weeks, months or years.

It's important at this stage to divide your goals into long term and short term goals. Having a mixture of both short term and long term goals helps maintain balance. For example, your long term '5 year goal' may be to become a pharmacy manager. But the short term will be to study for your upcoming exam.

Always have a mixture of short term and long term goals. Most students only focus on short term goals. But to be more effective you need to focus on both long term and short term goals.

3) <u>Find your inner drive</u>

From your list of goals, write down the top 5 goals which you are committed to achieving. Goals which massively improve your life.

"Instead of giving yourself reasons why you can't, give yourself reasons why <u>YOU CAN</u>"

If you have strong compelling reasons why you really want anything, you will be very passionate and resourceful and will find a way.

When I went back to university to study pharmacy, I had no money to pay my tuition fees. I did not know how I was going to pay for my pharmacy degree. I did not know how I would survive or where the money would come from, but I had very strong reasons for why I had to study pharmacy. My reasons were very compelling and they enabled me to overcome all challenges and obstacles to finally pay my way through university and get my degree.

Write down all the reasons why these goals are important to you and why you must achieve them.

4) Evidence of attainment

Now you have your top goals and your reasons for achieving them. Write down your evidence for attainment. How will you measure your success? What will you see, hear and feel once you start achieving your goal? For example; if your goal was to do well in your exams, your evidence may be seeing yourself reviewing your lecture notes daily, participating more in workshops, getting better grades in assessments and courseworks, making friends with other hard working students and explaining complex topics to other students.

5) Support network

"Alone we can do so little, together we can do so much".

You cannot accomplish any significant goal on your own. You will always need people to support you and resources. For example, if you want to get a first class degree, you may need support from some of your professors, or you may need to revise with certain friends that are outstanding and you may need certain books from the library.

Surround yourself with positive students, the doers, the believers and thinkers, but most of all, surround yourself with those who support you and see greatness within you, even when you don't see it yourself.

Make a list of all the resources you have and which ones you will need to achieve your goal, for example; friends, family, time, your character traits/ personality, education and unique sets of skills. Come up with a list of resources, skills, strengths and key people in your network who can help you achieve your goal.

6) <u>Look within yourself</u>

Review your internal resources by thinking of different situations where you have been successful or have achieved certain goals in the past, for example passing an exam, succeeding at an interview, losing weight and organising an event.

"Greatness exists in all of us".

Think of a few proud achievements in your life and recall what sort of personal skills and resources you used to achieve them. For example; were you more persistent? More focused? More determined? More motivated? More passionate?

Write them down. You will need these internal resources to achieve your goals again.

7) <u>Your identity</u>

For things to change around you, you have to change. To achieve certain goals, you'll have to change certain things about yourself or become a certain kind of person. You need to identify the sort of person you need to become to achieve your goal so that you have no internal conflicts.

Sometimes you need to sacrifice the person you are today to become the person you want to be tomorrow.

For example, if you want to run the marathon in a few months' time, you may need to change your eating habits. You may need to become proactive. You may need to develop certain qualities like being enthusiastic and positive, waking up early to train, changing your shopping and eating habits and working with a new set of friends.

What new skills do you need to develop to achieve your goals? Do you need to manage your time more effectively? Do you need to improve your communication skills? Do you have to be more outgoing? Do you need to learn new knowledge?

Most of us admire successful people. We admire great sporting heroes and celebrities, but we do not realise how much effort and hard work goes into developing their character to produce the results they produce.

We look at a Ronaldo, a Serena Williams, a Lewis Hamilton and we admire their skills and talent but we do not see the other components of success such as attitudes, persistence, beliefs and behaviours that go into shaping and producing their results.

Take some time now to write down a page of all the character traits, skills, beliefs and disciplines you will need to achieve your goals.

8) Change your story

"The only thing that stops you from getting what you want are the stories you tell yourself why you can't have it"

One of the reasons we fail to achieve our goals is because of the stories we tell ourselves. Stories like 'I'm not good enough' 'I don't have the time', 'I don't have the resources' 'I don't have the support' and 'people won't like me'. No matter how clear and motivated you are, if you do not overcome your obstacles you won't achieve your goals.

You must change your negative stories and beliefs, behaviours or personality traits which stop you from achieving your goals. Are you more scared of failing than succeeding? What are your fears? What is stopping you from taking action now? Are you too worried about what others think? Are you trying to satisfy everyone? Are you indecisive? Do you give up easily when things get tough? Are you scared of taking risks? Do you struggle to manage your time effectively?

Write down a list of all the things which you think stop you from achieving your goals, and commit to overcoming them. Overcome your fear, be courageous and act.

9) Find the right strategy

"Find a role model"

One of the quickest ways of achieving any goal is to find someone who is already producing the results that you want and then model them. Learn what they do and how they do it. A good role model can save you a lot of time and money. You can

27

learn successful strategies from role models on how to achieve your goals quickly.

For example, if your goal is to lose weight, then find one or two students who work out daily and look fit and healthy and learn their strategies.

Write down anyone who is already producing the result you want or who you can model. Focus on building relationships with these people or spend some time to meet them and get some advice and tips on how to reach your goals. They could also inspire and support you and teach you all the lessons they learnt along the way.

10) Design your perfect day

Create your ideal day. A day which represents a successful day towards achieving your goals.

Write down what your ideal day would involve. What will you do from the moment you wake up until you go to bed? Who will be involved? How will you spend the day? Where would you be? How would you feel at the end of your perfect day?

Write everything down and remember you must first see it in your mind to achieve it. Goals begin with a mental creation then a physical manifestation.

CHAPTER 4

Time Management

"The bad news is Time Flies. The good news is you're the pilot"

Do you sometimes feel overwhelmed by deadlines, courseworks, tests and assignments? Do you sometimes struggle to balance your studies and social life?

You are not alone. Time management is a common challenge for most students. It was a big challenge for me too. Time management requires self-discipline and self-mastery. My pharmacy degree was very demanding. I spent my mornings and afternoons attending lectures. I also worked part time in the evenings and I rarely had enough time to complete my courseworks and meet deadlines. I felt stressed most of the time.

I started studying pharmacy at the University of Bath in 2000. I completed my first year successfully but I wasn't keen on the amount of work I had to do daily. I was not very enthusiastic about Pharmacy. I envied my comrades who studied business courses and sometimes had only one or two lectures a week.

They always seemed to be very relaxed, partying hard, always having fun and enjoying their university experience, while I was always up early for lectures until dusk. I also spent a lot of sleepless nights in the library drinking unlimited cans of Red bull.

I was very discouraged, I struggled to manage my time and as a result I did not enjoy pharmacy and after completing my first year successfully, I switched to a degree in pharmaceutical management at the University of Bradford.

This was a management degree with a lot of variety to choose from. I enjoyed it more because I had less lectures and more flexibility. I had a lot of free time to socialise. I worked part time and I became the president of my university's African and Caribbean society. The role involved a lot of work in addition to studying for my degree. But it was a great experience for me at the time.

After obtaining my pharmaceutical management degree, I studied a lot of techniques on how to manage my time effectively. I became more competent and focused. After working for a few years, I returned to study pharmacy again, but this time at Kingston University in London. My pharmacy student experience was completely different this time from Bath. I participated in several extra-curricular activities and worked part time without my studies being affected.

I worked almost every evening in a call centre and every weekend. I also competed in several natural bodybuilding shows across the country and I won several trophies. I spent several hours in the gym daily preparing for competitions. In addition, I worked a few hours a week in an independent pharmacy to gain some pharmacy related work experience. I had a great social life, spent lots of time with friends, went out, partied and attended educational and social events.

The main reason I was able to enjoy my pharmacy experience in Kingston University more than I did at Bath was because I learnt how to manage my time effectively.

These skills have helped me become a successful pharmacy manager and superintendent pharmacist. I am in charge of a "100 hour" pharmacy. The pharmacy opens long hours from 7am -10:30pm, 7 days a week. It is extremely busy and does about 18,000 NHS items a month. I also manage about 20 staff members daily. Being a superintendent and pharmacy manager is very demanding and I spend a lot of hours at work each week.

I commute a long way to work, I spend 3 hours commuting daily. My shift patterns constantly change each week, alternating between late and early shifts. I also have two little girls who are very energetic and demand a lot of attention.

I make time to exercise and I go to the gym regularly. I spend a lot of time with my family, wife and kids. I am also an inspirational speaker and I travel frequently to various universities to deliver inspirational and motivational workshops to pharmacy students around the country. I am also a media pharmacist and I am actively involved in promoting pharmacy in the media and I organise and host several events over the year.

I recently won the runner up pharmacy manager award of the year for my company (community pharmacies). I am also an author and currently developing a lot of training programmes for pharmacy students and pharmacists.

So how have I managed to achieve all these things in such a short period of time? How do I manage to successfully balance everything? Spend time with my kids and family, spend time at work, spend time at the gym, spend time traveling around the country delivering motivational seminars, writing books and articles and winning awards?

The secret lies in my *time management skills*. These skills and techniques helped me to balance and manage my work load effectively at university, they helped me to succeed as a pre-reg student, pharmacy manager, superintendent, father, author, motivational speaker, media pharmacist and natural bodybuilding champion.

"All time management begins with planning"

In the next few pages you will discover the strategies and tools that helped me in the past and which continue to help me to achieve so much in such a short space of time, to be well balanced and always have extra time in the day.

I have learnt most of these time management techniques and philosophies from personal experience and from reading dozens of time management books and applying the principles.

I am very glad and excited to be sharing these with you because I am convinced that if you apply them like I did, you too will notice a significant improvement in your time management skills, you'll be able to maximise your time at university and produce outstanding results.

My Time Management Secrets

"Until we can manage time, we can manage nothing else"

1) Always create a 'To DO' list

Student life is very challenging. There are so many exams, assignments and courseworks to do. Your first step is to get a true picture of what you have to do. If you don't write things down, then you'll feel overwhelmed and stressed. You'll see things worse than they really are.

Making a to do list, or writing down on paper everything which you need to do gives you a clear and true picture of the outstanding things you need to accomplish.

One of my key principles is always to see things as they are and not worse than they are. I do this by creating a 'To Do' list.

Have you ever felt so stressed because you thought you had so much to do, but when you wrote everything down on paper, you realised it wasn't that bad? Writing down the things you have to do makes you feel better and gives you more control.

The goal is to make your 'to do' list as detailed and specific as you can. This empowers you to achieve things quicker. For example, instead of just writing down "read lecture notes" write down "read the first two cardiovascular topics of my physiology lecture for two hours in the morning and test myself for 45 mins".

The more specific you are, the more clarity and power you will have to achieve things. Assigning a date of completion and time duration enhances your possibilities and creates momentum to achieve more.

Below is an example of a 'to do' list which I used at university. It is very effective and has helped me to achieve a lot in little time. It helps me to stay focused and energised.

Number	Task	Due by?	Time duration	Done
1				
2				
3				
4				
5				
6				
7				

Exercise:

Complete the 'do to list' by entering all the various things you need to do. Assign a due date and time.

2) Student Planner

"Failing to plan is planning to fail"

A student planner is a very effective tool. I always created a planner at the start of each semester and reviewed it. It keeps you focussed and ahead of things. I had a clear view of everything I needed to do for the whole semester and as a result, I was always ahead of the game.

I failed to do this when I studied at Bath University and as a result, I procrastinated very often, I missed deadlines, I worked under pressure and completed important assignments at the last minute. I had sleepless nights and I was always unstable.

But when I discovered the planner, I used this at Kingston and I always completed my courseworks on time and I was more stable and relaxed despite being involved in a lot of activities.

The reason why the student planner is so effective and an incredible tool is because it gives you a forward and complete view of the whole semester. You can see your entire schedule for the next 4 months and plan accordingly. You can see busy periods in advance, periods where there are more deadlines, more assignments and more courseworks. It also highlights important social and academic events which you need to attend. For example; a family holiday or event which you need to attend. You will be more organised, more in control and focus on the priorities.

3) Weekly planner

I also found a weekly schedule extremely effective. When I was a student, I sometimes found it easier focusing on short term goals and so a weekly schedule is quite good.

Planning short term and long term is quite effective in managing your time. It prevents you spending sleepless nights trying to complete last minute deadlines or stressing before tests and exams. You will also notice that by planning both short term and long term, you will be able to optimise each study session with more understanding and see a general improvement in your grades.

A weekly planner improves your organisational skills because student life can be extremely busy and you can easily miss certain deadlines.

Let me share with you some tips on how to use your weekly planner to get the best out of your schedule and enhance your results.

Time	Mon	Tue	Wed	Thurs	Fri	Sat	sun
6-7am							
7-8am							
8-9am							
9-10am							
10-11am							
11-12							
12-1pm							
1-2pm							

2-3pm							
3-4pm							
4-5pm							
5-6pm							
6-7pm							
7-8pm							
8-9pm							
9-10pm							
10-11pm							

Tips to use your weekly planner effectively

1) Fill in all your academic lectures and workshops
2) Fill in all your personal/social commitments. For example; your leisure and sporting activities
3) Fill in family commitments
4) Fill in all your study/revision times, for example; times to read through your lectures daily and times to do assignments.

Make sure you enter all the important dates from your student planner into your weekly planner. Once you have blocked all this time, it gives you a clear idea of how much time you have left to study. Maximise this time and use it productively because this is the area that distinguishes your performance from other students.

Studies show that the human brain retains more information when we study in short bursts of 30-45 minutes as opposed to a 4 hour session in one sitting. You will be more effective if you spent 10 short (30 mins) study sessions with frequent breaks than 5 straight hours in one sitting with no breaks.

Identify how you can fully utilise short 30 min – 1 hour gaps in your planner. You can use these short sessions to review your lecture notes, do short readings, develop an essay or dissertation plan, and jot down notes from tutorials.

For longer time slots for example; 2 hours or more, review your notes in more detail. Read for courses, research topics, write assignments, revise for exams. To maintain your concentration, take frequent breaks and do not study for more than 45 mins without taking at least a 5- 10 min break.

Many students complain about making weekly schedules because they find it too rigid and want more flexibility. This is important. You need a balance so allow some flexibility and time for any unforeseen circumstances.

The key is to have a plan which allows you to make the most of your time whilst still giving you the flexibility for spontaneity and any unforeseen events. You do not need to be too rigid, this is just a guide. You can be flexible, you could decide to go workout one day rather than study. Or you may decide to go out for a meal with friends and reschedule a study period. The aim is for you to have control over the process and to enjoy it.

Be realistic with your plans. Do not cram too much into one day because you may fail to achieve your targets. This will affect your confidence and prevent you from planning in the future. For example; a plan to go to the gym directly after a long day of lectures, and then revise and go out partying later may be too much and as a result may affect your productivity. So make sure you are realistic with your planning.

Time management matrix

"Nobody is too busy, it's just a matter of priorities"

Have you ever been so busy but at the end of the day felt like you hadn't accomplished anything? Have you planned to do certain important activities but got interrupted by a friend or phone call which messed up your entire plans?

One of my greatest challenges as a student was learning how to prioritise my time effectively. How to avoid distractions and be extremely productive with my time.

Many times I would wake up early to revise but get distracted easily all day by either friends or phone calls. And at the end of the day I would stay up late trying to compensate for my poor time management in the day.

I was not effective until I discovered a very powerful time management matrix to prioritise my workload. I first came across this time management matrix when I read the late Dr Stephen Covey's book 'The 7 habits of highly effective people".

When I discovered this matrix, it completely changed the way I prioritised my workload. I focused more on achieving the things that mattered most and I avoided distractions. I became a lot more productive, focussed and in control. I realised that nobody is too busy, it's just a matter of priorities.

The time management matrix helped me learn how to prioritise tasks in order of *urgency* and *importance*. I realised that not all urgent tasks are important tasks. It helped me to decide whether to attend to something straight away or to do it later. For example; whilst studying, your phone ringing is urgent because it needs your immediate attention, however, it is not important as you can ignore the call, finish studying then return the call later.

The time management matrix is separated into four quadrants as illustrated below. The quadrants are divided in terms of importance and urgency. You need to be able to distinguish which tasks are important and which ones are urgent for you. You also need to be clear on those activities which are within your control and those that are outside of your control.

Time management matrix

Quadrant 1	*Quadrant 2*
IMPORTANT	**IMPORTANT**
&	**&**
URGENT	**NOT URGENT**
Quadrant 3	*Quadrant 4*
	NOT IMPORTANT
NOT IMPORTANT	**&**
&	**NOT URGENT**
URGENT	

Important: Important activities focus primarily on you. They are mainly your personal goals and things which you want to achieve.

Urgent: Urgent activities require immediate attention. They are pressured activities, the "do it now" activities. They are usually linked to other people, the accomplishment of other people's goals or demands. If you don't deal with them immediately then there could be several implications.

Summary of what each quadrant means

1) *Quadrant 1*: Important deadlines with high urgency. The first quadrant contains tasks and responsibilities that need immediate attention.

2) *Quadrant 2*: Long term planning.

   This quadrant is for activities that are important but do not need to be done straight away. This quadrant should be used for strategic planning and long term execution.

3) *Quadrant 3:* Distractions with high urgency.

   This quadrant is reserved for tasks that are urgent, but not necessarily important. These activities should be eliminated or minimised as they are not productive. They can be delegated to others.

4) *Quadrant 4:* Activities with little or no value.

   This quadrant focuses on tasks that do not yield any value. Activities which are not important and not urgent. These are time wasters and should be eliminated at all costs.

What quadrants do most of your daily activities fall into? Before I discovered the time matrix, most of my activities were in quadrant 1 and 3. If this is the same for you, then you need to rethink the way you prioritise your time. To get maximum benefits, the majority of your activities should fall into quadrant 2. This is the area where you have more control and more planning. Activities in this quadrant are important but not urgent and as a result you have a more balanced and highly productive outcome. If you have very few activities in this quadrant, then it means you focus more on being reactive to circumstances rather than being proactive.

If you can get most of your activities in quadrant 2 before they become quadrant 1 activities then you will be a lot more balanced, stable and productive at university or college. It's easy to mistake activity for productivity. It's easy to think and feel you are very busy. The question is "Busy doing what?" Is what you are doing today getting you closer to where you want to be tomorrow?

Let's look at each quadrant in more detail below.

"Either you run the day, or the day runs you" Jim Rohn

Quadrant 1- urgent and important

There are two types of activities that fall into this quadrant. Some are unforeseen activities. These are emergencies which occur out of the blue and you have no direct control or influence over them and you need to act on them urgently. For example; a family emergency.

The second type of activities in this quadrant are those that you have more control over. Those urgencies that could be prevented through planning and effective time management. They are mainly activities which were in quadrant 2 but were ignored or mismanaged and have now become quadrant 1. For example; coursework deadlines which have been ignored until the night before the deadline.

The first quadrant should mainly have unforeseen emergencies, activities which are out of your control and not those that have come from quadrant 2. For example;

- Crises
- Unexpected emergencies

Quadrant 2- not urgent but important

Most students overlook this area and ignore it. If this area is not well managed, these activities become quadrant 1 (urgent) activities. This area requires planning and should be your target quadrant as a student. Most students tend to focus simply on urgent tasks and postpone important ones until they become urgent. We focus on the 'here and now' and ignore the future. Activities in this quadrant involve important areas in life such as your health, your career, exercise, family, personal development. These activities give you a sense of fulfilment. And if ignored will become a quadrant 1 activity later. For instance, reading lecture notes daily after each lecture is important but not urgent, so most students ignore this activity until exams or tests are due and they get stressed and eventually burn out.

Another example is exercising and eating healthily. Most of us know it is important to exercise and eat healthily daily but it is not urgent. Thus we ignore it until we get a health problem then exercising and eating healthily becomes urgent.

Investing time in this area may not be urgent but in the long term it will be of utmost importance. If you focus enough time in this quadrant you will be more balanced, you will complete your work and deadlines on time. This should be your time management goal and desired quadrant for the majority of your activities to be successful at university, college and beyond. The reason most students have less activities in this quadrant is because it requires, self-discipline and self-control.

Examples of activities in this quadrant are;

- Planning (academic, social & financial)
- Preparing
- Self-development and investment
- Exercise, health, recreation

Quadrant 3: urgent but not important

These activities are urgent activities but not important and do not contribute towards achieving your personal goals. They are mostly ego-driven activities and are better delegated to someone else or rescheduled. For example; if a friend or colleague is requesting for a quadrant 3 activity you can politely decline their request, or ask them to reschedule for another time as it does not contribute anything towards your wider goals.

Examples of quadrant 3 activities are;

- Interruptions (phone calls, texts, emails)
- Meetings
- Appointments

Quadrant 4: not urgent and not important

This is a quadrant you must avoid as much as possible. Activities in this quadrant do not contribute any value to your goals, they are time wasters and should be avoided. Students who spend a lot of time in this area, usually have poor grades, regularly miss deadlines and have no real focus or sense of planning. As a result, they are underachievers at university or college.

All activities in this quadrant are nothing but distractions and you need to distance yourself from them if you want to be successful.

Despite being irrelevant and absolute time wasters, these activities tend to be the most entertaining, hence most students participate in them for many hours without noticing. Many student activities lie in this area, because unlike quadrant 2 activities, these require no self-discipline, no planning, no focus and no self-control. You just go where ever the wind blows.

Examples of activities in this quadrant include

- Surfing the internet without purpose
- Watching unnecessary TV programmes for several hours
- Constantly on social media, Viber, Facebook, Snapchat, LinkedIn, WhatsApp for long hours

How to apply the matrix to your degree/course

Your goal is to maximise the matrix and your productivity by concentrating the majority of your efforts on quadrant 2 activities. This will give you a more structured and balanced approach to life at university or college. It will eliminate unnecessary stress and worry and will lead to tremendous success.

The main question to consider when using this matrix, is "Does the activity bring you closer to your goal or not?"

CHAPTER 5

<u>Study tips for exams</u>

Another big challenge for most students is preparing for exams. What study tips and techniques can help you excel? How can you maximise your revision time? In this chapter, I will introduce you to 14 study tips to help you succeed at any exam. These techniques are well researched and if applied are guaranteed to produce outstanding results. I applied them throughout my studies and they have helped me to succeed.

1) Study time

How long should study sessions last?

Research shows that we retain information better in small chunks than big ones. You will retain more information if you study at short regular intervals. For example; it's more effective to do 10 short regular '30 mins' study sessions than a straight 5 hr session. Ideally, 45 mins-1 hr revision sessions with regular breaks have been shown to be most effective. Regular breaks will also boost your productivity and improve your focus.

2) Electronic vs hardcopy

Should you study directly from a laptop or lecture handouts?

Many students study directly from their IPads or laptops. When I was at university, I studied several times directly from my laptop. Computers, tablets and all sorts of e-learning formats are good, but research shows that you retain information quicker by reading directly from a lecture handout than an electronic copy. Reading time is slower with an IPad than handouts.

A study by a psychology lecturer from Leicester University found that students who read the same information from a computer had to read several times to fully absorb the information compared to students who read the information from lecture handouts.

Print out all lecture notes and avoid studying directly from IPads, laptops or computers.

3) Your study Environment

Where should you study for the best results?

Studies show that studying the same information in different places each day improves memory. Every time you move to a new place to study the same material, you activate new associations which improve memory. I used to read in different places during my degree and I noticed that I absorbed and retained more when I changed environment.

When you revise, make sure you study the same information in different places such as; the library, class rooms, bedrooms and even outdoors to improve retention.

4) Test yourself

A study in a science magazine showed that students who tested themselves after learning a subject retained 50% more information a week later, than students who did not test themselves. It's important to test yourself with as many past papers as possible. Challenge and test your understanding with friends to be fully prepared and understand information better. Do as many practise papers as possible and test yourself after learning each new topic.

5) Avoid distractions

A study by the University of Indiana showed that distractions such as, texting or using social media while studying reduce brain efficiency as they interfere with the absorbing and processing of information.

One of our biggest distractions are our mobile phones. It is amazing how much information you can absorb and retain when you avoid distractions. I noticed a great improvement in my revision sessions and understanding on the days when I turned off my mobile phone when revising, compared to the days when I did not.

My best advice will be to turn your mobile phone off when studying and check it during your breaks to maximise your efficiency.

6) Study to the 'Beat'

Should you listen to music while studying?

By music, I don't mean 'Justin Beiber' or "Eminem". Classical music has been shown to stimulate brain waves which activate memory.

Download some Pandora and play it while studying. Hans Zimmer's Pandora study music is a favourite and helps engage the brain. Try it.

7) Make the connections

Tony Buzzan, author of Mind Maps, showed that quick learners make connections between ideas as opposed to merely memorising them.

Learn actively by making connections and associations with any new material you learn. The best tool I have found from my experience for making connections is learning to use mind maps.

Mind maps are an incredible tool for activating all parts of your brain and improving learning and retention capacity.

8) Supercharge your brain

Several studies have shown the benefits of exercising and how it improves concentration, focus and performance. According to Dr Douglas Mckeag, from the University of Indiana, exercise gets blood flowing into your brain, oxygenates it and increases your alertness and mental capacity.

Here is a tip which worked for me at university. Before you start revising, do some light exercise, brisk walk, jog, dance, jump, run or do some push ups for a few minutes, this will activate your brain capacity as you increase the flow of oxygen to it.

9) Feed your brain

What should you eat before an exam?

Studies show that eating a healthy balanced diet and keeping yourself hydrated is essential for brain function. In a study, students who took water with them to exams were more alert than those who did not.

There is a library of evidence on the benefits of fish oil for brain activity and nutrients such as omega 3, 6 and 9.

Ensure you eat a balanced diet, a good amount of fish, nuts, avocados, almonds and olive oil in the weeks leading to your exam and keep yourself hydrated. A good combination of omega 3, 6 & 9 can be found in the fantastic Udo's Oil.

Do not forget to take some water with you to every exam. Always keep yourself hydrated during revision sessions.

10) Note taking

What is the best way to make notes?

Flashcards are best for active recall. Studies have shown the 'Leitner System' to be very effective in helping recall information quicker. This system also helps you review material which you don't know over and over until you memorise it fully.

11) Study time

When is the best time to study?

There isn't really a best time to study, it all depends on the individual, but studies show that our brains form new connections when we are asleep.

You will therefore process and retain information better if you read new information just before going to bed as opposed to in the day when you have more distractions. But study times vary, some people study better in the mornings, some afternoons, some evenings and others at night. Find out what works best for you and stick to it.

12) Reviewing lecture notes

When is the best time to review lecture notes?

Researchers have demonstrated that the first time you hear a lecture or study something new, if you review the material that same day within 24 hrs, you retain up to 80% of what you learnt. If you did this, then a week later it will only take 5 minutes of revising to retain 100%.

Review your lecture notes on the same day of the lecture to retain it long term.

13) Teach it

The best way to learn something is to teach it. A study separated students into two groups. One group was asked to study the topic to take a test at the end, while the other group was asked to study the same topic but to teach it to colleagues at the end. Students who were asked to teach the topic understood the topic better than those who only read it for the test.

Get together with friends and perform various role plays. Act as a teacher and teach each topic you learn. When you learn to teach a subject you activate your brain at a deeper level creating an in depth understanding. You will also get positive insights from colleagues.

14) Study with A+ students

Most of the outstanding results I got at university were as a result of studying with other hard working and intelligent students. Most were more intelligent than me and they challenged me to work harder.

Join a good study group, or a network of hardworking students to guarantee outstanding results.

CHAPTER 6

Health & Vitality

"Your health is your wealth"

As a personal trainer and someone who has always been keen on my health and nutrition, I always get certain questions asked all the time. How do you have so much energy to do all you do?

How do you run a 100 hr pharmacy? Travel around the country delivering motivational seminars? Spend time with family and raising two children, get time to exercise and work out daily, work long hours and still be filled with so much energy.

This next chapter is very important and is probably the most important because I believe energy is everything. Our personal energy is the fuel of our life. Everything we do or achieve is based on our energy levels, the actions we take, the results we produce, our emotions and thoughts are all controlled and dictated by our energy levels.

I was always fascinated by one question, "how can I create and sustain an optimum amount of energy daily and maintain my health and fitness?"

I tried several diets, several ideas on optimum health and nutrition. One thing I noticed as I researched different diets, different nutrition topics was that I found out there is a lot of controversy. The moment you read all the incredible research of the positivity of one diet or certain nutritional principles, within a few minutes you'll be reading evidence which contradicts all the research.

So when it comes to your health and nutrition, I personally developed one method and approach and its 'Try and experience things for yourself'. I realised that my experience was my best evidence. I decided to try eating certain foods and I adopted certain health and nutrition practices and I discovered which ones gave me the greatest energy and vitality, not only in my body, but my general wellbeing and kept me healthy.

I experimented with different foods and saw which ones worked best for me. If you feel and experience something, you have a stronger conviction and belief than if you just acted based on someone else's belief.

So over these next pages, I will share with you the principles I have applied and continued to apply to have abundant energy on a daily basis and also stay healthy without illness or imbalance.

I only discovered these when I tried them and then I noticed the effects they had on me. I ate more of the foods that made me feel energetic and revitalised and less of those that made me feel the opposite regardless of the taste.

I had to change my mind set from eating for pleasure to eating for optimum health and performance. When you change your mind in this way, you begin to appreciate the simplicity of nutrition and life's true balance. You'll wake up in the mornings feeling energised, balanced and strong.

The first thing I discovered was in order to maintain your health and your body effectively, it's important to understand how it works and what puts your body out of balance? It's important to understand our body environment. Just like with everything in life, I believe there are universal laws. Our bodies are designed to function optimally within the application of certain laws and deviating from these lead to imbalance and the development of several bodily complications and poor health.

For example, I remember one Saturday afternoon when I was taking my wife and kids to my friend's daughter's birthday party in London. We were very late and I was rushing to get home after work so we could all leave before the rush hour.

We left the house in a rush and I stopped at the petrol station and quickly filled my car with fuel. It was a diesel car and unfortunately because I was rushing and I was in such a state, I filled it up with petrol instead. I did not realise this until I started driving.

The car felt a bit funny, it wasn't driving normally and something didn't feel right. I continued to drive the car for about 10 mins and we got to a very big roundabout, as I drove into the roundabout on this very busy afternoon with so much traffic, the car immediately stopped and my engine switched off.

I then realised I had put in £70 worth of petrol, the wrong fuel in my diesel car. The petrol had clogged the whole engine, my car could not function and the engine ceased immediately. We were all in a state as we stopped just by the exit of a roundabout at a point which was not very visible to oncoming drivers and it was a very dangerous position.

We could not also leave the vehicle because at the pace the traffic was coming we did not have enough time to get both kids out from the back and even leave the roundabout. We were stuck in this dangerous position with my kids crying at the back and I called the police who managed to divert the traffic and get us out of the roundabout to safety. I called a fuel doctor who arrived 6 hours later and removed all the petrol from the tank.

At the end we did not attend the party, I lost some money, I put my entire family at risk and my engine stopped working. This all happened because I put the wrong fuel type.

The same principle applies to our bodies. If we do not follow the natural fuel which our bodies are designed to have and we put in alternatives or incompatible types of fuel, we will clog up our biological system leading to organ failure, poor health, disease and even death.

BODY BALANCE

In order to optimise your health you need to understand your body's natural environment.

The best way to maintain this fine balance and to experience this rejuvenation and vitality is simple. Eat natural foods as much as possible. Make sure you have vegetables with most of your meals. Avoid eating processed foods.

I found it a bit challenging at first sticking to eating certain foods as I was not really a big fan of vegetables, but when I noticed the positive effects on my body, the energy and balance I felt, I realised it was worth it. Figuring out how to make the right food choices is a great start on your quest for success and peak performance. It's important to become aware which foods drain your energy and put your health at risk and which ones empower you and keep you strong and healthy.

I had to make certain choices and a few healthy food substitutions. The more natural you eat, the more energised you will feel. Create and maintain a more alkali internal environment rather than an acidic one.

7 Tips to improve your health & vitality

1) <u>Ditch 'coffee'</u>

   Most of us enjoy several cups of coffee, tea or energy drinks daily. Especially in the mornings or when we stay up all right revising for tests or exams or working towards deadlines. I use to drink several cans of red bull and relentless at university until I realised the side effects of too much coffee. I realised that when I swapped caffeine for de-caffeinated drinks I felt a lot more energetic and emotionally balanced.

Most of us do not realise the health risks associated with too much caffeine. Too much caffeine has been shown to raise blood pressure, increase heart attacks in young adults, cause insomnia, indigestion, headaches and affects pregnancy leading to birth abnormalities.

Substitute caffeinated drinks for de-caffeinated or more natural options and you'll notice a significance increase in your health and vitality.

2) Work' it'

I can't stress the importance of exercising regularly at university or whilst studying. We all know of the benefits of exercising but many students don't exercise because they link pain to exercising. Exercising is the key to creating an unstoppable flow of energy within you. Motion creates emotion and the more active you are, the better you'll feel. Exercise is the miracle cure we've always had, it's a free cure, but when we neglect to take the recommended dose, we suffer the consequences. If you take good care of your body for the early years of your life, it will take care of you for later years.

The health benefits of exercising are endless. Studies have shown that exercising increases your brains capacity and mental alertness. You'll absorb information better, study better and excel in your exams and course works when you exercise. You will continuously put your body in a peak mental and physical state for peak performance.

People who do regular exercise have a lower risk of many long term conditions such as diabetes, heart disease, stroke and some cancers. Research shows that physical activity can boost your self-esteem, mood, sleep, energy levels, reduce stress and make you feel healthier and happier.

Take exercising seriously if you want you live a good quality of life as you get older. Try to be active daily and perform at least 2 hours of moderate activity each week. Moderate activity includes activities that can raise your heart rate and you can still hold a conversation whilst doing them without running out of breath, for example; brisk walking, swimming and cycling. However, the more you do the better you'll look and the healthier you'll feel.

3) Bin the 'late meals'

Most students enjoy eating late at night after a night out or as a result of staying up very late. Eating late at night especially just before going to bed can leave you feeling bloated and suffer from acid reflux. Avoid spicy and fatty foods especially late at night. During the night our metabolism is lower because we are less active. When you eat late, most of your food is stored as fat, hence the reason why most students who eat late at night gain weight faster. Our digestion process also requires a lot of energy and interrupts sleep. Most students struggle to sleep properly and suffer from indigestion when they eat very late or eat heavy meals just before going to bed.

I use to suffer a lot from reflux at university until I stopped eating late meals. The secret is to eat something light in the evening and eat your last meal 3-4 hours before going to bed. You'll be more energetic and vibrant when you wake up in the morning.

4) Quit smoking

We know smoking is one of the biggest causes of death in the world. Every year around 100,000 people in the UK die from smoking and many living with smoking related illnesses such as COPD. Smoking causes about 90% of lung cancers and many other cancers. It damages your heart and increases your risk of heart disease and strokes. It has also been shown to cause birth defects, miscarriages and low birth baby weight. There are many students who smoke at university, if you are one of them, then you want to consider quitting early if you can. I encourage you to enrol on a stop smoking programme or get some support to kick this habit before it is too late.

5) Give up the 'Booze''

This is one of the hardest areas to write about because some students would say there is no student life without alcohol. It's all about binge drinking and partying hard. It also doesn't help on student nights when alcoholic drinks are a lot cheaper. It's all fun getting drunk on a night out but thinking about your health is also important. Avoid alcoholic drinks in general if you can, but if you must drink then avoid consuming more than 14 units (6 pints of average-strength beer) a week, if you do then you are putting your health at risk. Many links have been made between drinking and illnesses such as cancer. There was evidence at some point that a small amount of alcohol is good for the heart, but that evidence has now been revised.

If you drink more than 14 units a week then within 10-20 years, studies show that you may develop mouth, throat and breast cancer, stroke, heart disease, liver and brain damage. The effects on your health will depend on how much you consume, the less you consume, the lower the risk.

Most students enjoy binge drinking, but drinking too much, too quickly in a single session causes all sorts of problems including low self-control, unprotected sex, accidents from injury, misjudging risks and in some situations death.

Avoid drinking alcohol completely if you can or consume within the limits and do not binge drink. Drink slowly and drink with food not on an empty stomach. Alternate with water and non-alcoholic drinks from time to time to break the cycle.

6) Stop eating 'on the go'

Student life can be very stressful at times. Sometimes you barely have a minute for yourself and drained with endless deadlines and course works. Stress, anxiety and eating meals very quickly have a very negative effect on our digestive systems. Most students eat on the go, in between lectures.

A study published by the Journal of the American Dietetic Association found women aged between 30-40 who ate the quickest are more likely to be obese than slow eaters. Eating too fast overrides signals that tell our brain we are full. When you eat too quickly, you are likely to over eat. Eating too fast also causes many indigestion problems, bloating and flatulence. Take your time when eating, be calm and do not rush your meals to optimise your digestive system and your health.

7) Water & water rich foods

We already know about the benefits of water but most students stay dehydrated and do not consume enough water daily. Our body is more than 60% water. Not carbonated drinks, not tea, not coffee not highly marketed water substitutes, just pure water.

Water is the key component that maintains all our cells, organs and systems and keep us alive. Our functioning and body balance depends on it. Water is our body's fuel. Most of us do not drink enough water and there are many health risks to dehydration. Majority of the population knows about the benefits of drinking water, but very few know about the importance of also consuming water rich foods

Approximately 20% of our hydration is meant to come from food. If you are not drinking enough water daily and consuming water rich foods, then you are straining your body and putting your health at risk.

Drinking water daily and consuming water rich foods has several health benefits including lubricating soft tissues preventing joint pain, congestion and muscle cramps. Water transports all the nutrients throughout our body. It cleanses and detoxifies our system. Our saliva is vital for digestion and water is its main component. Water is a natural appetite suppressant, it increases your fat burning capacity and helps to maintain a healthy weight or weight loss.

Water cleanses or organs, it flushes toxins from our liver and kidneys. People who drink more water have a lower risk of kidney stones, urinary tract infections and constipation. Dehydration causes ageing, it triggers the formation of wrinkles. One of the quickest ways to look young and healthy is to drink a lot of water throughout the day.

Very important is the fact that our brain is 90% water and requires more oxygen than any other organ in our body to function. Hence water increases our mental capacity and can boost our performance at university. Dehydration can cause dizziness, irritability, mood swings and imbalance. Many headaches or hangovers are a result of dehydration.

Here is my advice to stay hydrated, drink water regularly throughout the day and also consume vegetables and fruits with each meal. This will help you stay hydrated. Water rich foods include water melons, cranberries, strawberries, apples and grapes. For vegetables; cucumber, celery, lettuce, tomato, green garbage and broccoli.

CHAPTER 7

Job applications & interview tips

Several years ago, I struggled with job applications, writing CVs and performing well at interviews. I was not confident and I got rejected countless times.

It all changed when I met a career advisor called Roy Christian. I met Roy when I was studying at the University of Bradford. She was a great lady and worked with the Impact Project. Impact was a positive action project for black and minority ethnic students. Roy also worked with students whose families had no previous experience of higher education or of accessing the graduate job market. It was a project which equipped minority ethnic students with the tools and techniques to excel at job interviews and job applications

Roy Christian was extremely passionate, supportive and caring. I credit her for most of my career confidence and success today. I would not be where I am today without her. She had a direct approach. The first day I met Roy was at a job interview appointment. I gave her my CV which I had spent three weeks writing. I was very proud and knew I had the 'best' CV in the world.

I gave my CV to Roy to look at and give me some feedback. I was very proud and had a huge grin on my face because I was convinced she would be impressed. She looked at my CV for about 30 seconds, sighed, tore the CV in front of me and threw it in the bin and said "this is rubbish".

I was shocked and outraged. I had just met this lady for the first time and I did not like her. I felt offended and my ego was hurt. But at the same time I was curious to know why she did not like 'the best' CV in the world. She asked me to send her a copy of my CV electronically and she would redo it for me and show me an example of what a good CV should look like. I was very upset and left her office. I sent her the electronic copy. She asked me to come to her office the next day.

I went to see her the next day very reluctantly. As I walked into her office, she presented me with a rough guide of my re-edited CV and what a good CV should look like. As soon as I looked at the CV, I was blown away. I was speechless. The style, design and the way she formatted my CV was incredible. I was very impressed and I decided she would be my career coach instantly.

The next section is filled with incredible knowledge and insights that I learnt from Roy Christian, everything she taught me. Roy has impacted the lives of hundreds of students. Through her knowledge, advice and skills many students have succeeded at interviews and had high profile jobs. I gained a lot of confidence and she has had a huge impact on my career.

Here are the secrets of interview and job application success that I have learnt from Roy.

SKILLS FOR SUCCESS

There are certain key skills which you must develop as a student if you want to succeed. These are the key skills I learnt from Roy and the positive behaviours associated with them. I spent several years developing and enhancing these skills or competencies. Focus on developing these skills and you will be brilliant and excel at job interviews.

Skills/Competencies
(Positive characteristic behaviours associated with success)

Adaptability/Flexibility
- Keeps an open mind to new ways of doing things
- Adapts effectively to new learning opportunities and situations
- Tailors own style and approach to fit specific goals/projects
- Takes a flexible approach to modifying plans to achieve objectives within appropriate constraints

Analytical Skills/Problem Solving

- Pays attention to detail but can also see the bigger picture
- Can think outside the box
- Produces creative solutions to problems/situations generating a range of novel alternatives
- Analyses information systematically, rapidly extracting relevant data
- Gets to the heart of a problem identifying root causes
- Generates options and possible solutions, uses intuitive thinking to solve problems
- Adopts appropriate level of analysis
- Breaks problems down to logical, manageable components

Communication Skills
- Listens to what others have to say
- Encourages 2-way exchange of information
- Speaks clearly
- Tailors approach to suit the audience
- Ensures written documents are presented clearly, succinctly and accurately

Creativity and Innovation

- Generates new ideas and approaches
- Responds positively to new ways of working or changes in objectives
- Keeps an open mind to new ways of doing things
- Adapts effectively to new learning opportunities and situations

Customer Service Focus

- Demonstrates a strong customer orientation (internal and external)
- Ensures all activities add value
- Maintains an awareness of competitor activity
- Takes time to understand customer needs
- Builds relationships with customers

Influencing and Negotiating

- Listens to what others have to say, acknowledging new information
- Influences a 2-way exchange of information
- Negotiates to achieve key objective outcomes in return for concessions on non-key objectives
- Sells the benefits of a course of action or ideas to others
- Quickly connects and establishes rapport with customers, colleagues and superiors

Information Handling

- Attention to detail
- Identifies relevant sources of information and seeks further information if required
- Analyses information systematically, rapidly extracting relevant data
- Accurately interprets numerical and verbal information

Initiative
- Uses own initiative to actively influence events
- Proactively looks for opportunities to contribute

Judgement
- Extracts relevant information from different data sources
- Focuses on key issues
- Weighs up the pros and cons of an issue
- Knows who and when to consult
- Anticipates questions and arguments
- Considers the implications of what might be done and said
- Delivers practical solutions

Planning and Organising
- Looks ahead, identifying future developments and evaluating implications for own plans
- Prioritises work carefully
- Fully utilises the resources available
- Sets targets and milestones and monitors progress against them
- Monitors progress against plans so can act accordingly
- Has contingency plans in place

Resilience/Working Under Pressure
- Demonstrates enthusiasm
- Has a positive, can do attitude
- Remains calm in the face of setbacks/pressure

Results Driven
- Takes responsibility for their own work
- Sets targets and aims to exceed them
- Demonstrates enthusiasm and interest in the pursuits of goals
- Goes the extra mile to achieve

Team Work

- Actively participates
- Asks others for their views
- Encourages/supports contributions from others
- Responds positively to requests for help
- Seeks common ground
- Keen to work with others from different functions
- Shares information
- Interacts in a sensitive way
- Proactively develops relationships with others
- Dedicates time to identifying and networking with key individuals

Competencies, descriptions & interview questions

1) Motivation

Motivation is about pushing yourself and others to perform well in the job. It is about achieving satisfaction from doing a job well and being goal oriented.

Positive Behaviours
• Understands importance of role and how it fits into the wider scheme of things
• Is conscientious and takes pride in work at all times
• Is constantly looking for ways to improve working practices
• Is constantly looking for ways to improve personal performance
• Takes a proactive approach to work

Examples of motivation questions

1) Can you tell me about a time when you had a very boring or tedious piece of work to do? What did you do to make sure you stayed motivated while doing the work?

    - What was the work?
    - Why did you find it boring?
    - What did you do?
    - Why did you do that?

2) Can you tell me about a time when you have been really pleased with something you did at work?

    a. What was it?
    b. Why were you pleased?
    c. Who else noticed?
    d. What was their reaction?

3) Describe a situation where you have worked hard and felt proud of your achievement.

2) Customer Focus

Customer focus is about understanding what customer's value and taking responsibility for delivering an excellent service

Positive Behaviours
• Takes personal responsibility for meeting customer needs
• Diffuses angry/annoyed customers effectively
• Deals with complex customer requirements
• Is prepared to go the extra mile for the customer
• Exceeds customer expectations – gets compliments to prove it.

Questions:

What experience do you have of providing customer services in your current or previous role?

- How much contact did/do you have with customers?
- What was your role?
- What did you enjoy?

a) Can you give me an example of an occasion when you felt that you provided a piece of good customer service?

- What was your role?
- What did you do?
- How did the customer respond?
- How did you know they were happy?

b) Can you tell me about a time when you have dealt with a customer who was unhappy with the service that they received?

- What was your role?
- Why was the customer unhappy?
- What did you do?
- What was the outcome?

3) Team Working:

Team working is about being able to work as part of a team and building relationships with other team members. It is about enjoying the team aspects and being able to contribute effectively to team goals

Positive Behaviours
• Recognises strengths and weaknesses in others and self
• Is an enthusiastic contributor to the team cause
• Takes responsibility for a designated part of the project
• Enjoys working with others
• Understands the importance of good inter-team relationships

Questions:

a) Can you tell me about a situation where you have been part of a group working towards a specific goal?
   - What was your role?
   - What was the goal?
   - What did you do to help?
   - How did you decide what to do?
   - What was the result?

b) What aspects of your work, have involved working with others?

   - What was your role?
   - What did you most enjoy and why?
   - What did you least enjoy and why?
   - What problems did you encounter?
   - How did you deal with them?

4) Organisational skills

Planning and organising is about effective organising and prioritising workload and being able to cope under pressure in a difficult situation.

Positive Behaviours
• Is able to prioritise work with little or no guidance
• Informs people of any potential over run
• Asks people for guidance when deciding which tasks are the most important
• Organises time and workload efficiently to get all the work completed
• Plans tasks in advance to meet deadlines

Questions:

a) Can you tell me about a time when an urgent task has forced you to re-think your priorities?
   - What was the urgent task?
   - What were your original priorities?
   - Why did they change?
   - How did you decide what to do?
   - What happened in the end?

b) Can you tell me about a time when you have had several things to do at the same time? How did you manage to make sure they were all completed properly?
   - What were the tasks?
   - How did you know which were the most important?
   - Who did you speak to?
   - What did you do?
   - What happened?

c) Describe a situation where you have planned and organised an event, project or activity, which involved a fixed deadline. How successful was the result?

5) Communication skills

Ensures that the message is clear and understood

Positive Behaviours
• Self confidence in communicating style
• Was able to show evidence of relating to others easily
• Listens, asks questions if unsure and checks understanding

Questions:

a) Give an example of when you have had to explain something to someone. How did you ensure they understood you?

b) Tell me about a time when you have not understood what someone was telling you.
   - What did you do?
   - What was the result?
   - What could you have done differently?

Competency Based Interview Tips & Techniques

<u>Competency</u>

A competence is a set of skills, knowledge and behaviours which enable you to perform a given task successfully. It is a group of positive behaviours organised in a specific way to produce an outcome. For example, if you are competent training new staff then you possess a set of skills, knowledge and behaviours which allow you to successfully train them.

Why are competency based interviews important?

Competency based interviews allow employers to determine what skills you have which can be transferred to the business to make a significant contribution. They give an indication of your ability and capability.

Examples of competency based questions

- Describe a time when you have encountered a problem and developed a process to improve it. Describe the situation/background and what was your role? What actions did you take and why? What was the outcome?

- Describe a time when you have worked in a team to overcome an obstacle and achieve a common goal. Describe the situation and your role. How did you communicate with the team? How did the team resolve the issue?

Tips to succeed at competency based interviews

1. Listen & dissect the question

Take time to reflect on each competency question you are asked at interview. Do not rush into answering without clearly listening to the question and then breaking it down. Think clearly about what the employer is looking for in each question and why you are being asked the question.

Remember it is always about the employer and your answers must always be linked to the company directly or indirectly. For example, think carefully about this question and why an employer would ask this question.

Describe a time when you worked effectively as part of a team to achieve a goal, what was your role and what did you do?

2. Choose the right example

"The quality of your answers at any competency interview is based on the quality of examples you choose"

Always choose the right examples which will demonstrate your skills, knowledge and attitude. The example you choose could determine your success or failure at an interview.

Here are some tips to choose the right examples

- Give recent examples (3 years or less)
- Give examples which demonstrate a wide number of skills and competencies in that area.

- Choose examples from employment (part time jobs or voluntary work), academic (course projects) extracurricular activities (voluntary, work, societies, recreational, sports) and personal stories.

- You can give examples from any of these areas and most employers prefer a mixture of examples from different areas to add variety and also express more areas of your personality.

  However, always make sure you choose the right area which is relevant to the job you are applying for. For example, it will be more appropriate to choose an example from a part time customer service job rather than from an academic project for a customer service question.

- Give a range of different examples from different areas. For example, many employers commented that 99% of students give examples mainly from "Doing a group project at university" when asked about team work. Choosing different examples from different areas of your life will give you the edge over other students and will add variety to your answers and make you more appealing to interviewers.

- Use different examples to demonstrate each competence, do not use the same example unless your interviewers ask you to.

How to answer competency based interview questions

There are different ways to answer competency based questions. The most effective strategy I use is called S.B.O (Situation Behaviour Outcome), some people call it the STAR technique (Situation Task Action results).

This strategy helps you present your answers in a very structured and organised way. It also keeps you focused on the question and enables you to provide the most appropriate and relevant details.

Let me illustrate the S.B.O strategy with an example;

Think of the following question.

Describe a *situation* where you have worked as part of a team. (This is asking you to describe the **situation**)

What was your role? What did you do? How did you overcome challenges? (this is asking you to describe your **behaviour**)

What was the **outcome?**

- Each question (such as above) can be answered by using the same approach as shown below. The percentages (in brackets), are shown as a guide and as approximations only.

a) **Situation (~15 – 20%)**

- Here, you set the scene in order to describe your behaviour in the particular scenario.

- What was going on? What was the problem?

b) Behaviour (~60 - 70%) – Your specific contribution

- The spot light is on you in this area. It's all about you and the specific actions or contributions you made. This is where you highlight all your skills, behaviours and attitudes. It is the most important part of your answer.

- *Be specific and stay focused on you, not others – say what YOU did, not what "Tom or John" or "we" did.*

- Quantify/qualify your statements/answers

  For example;
  I was responsible for handling and resolving up to 100 queries per day. I was handling cash and credit transactions of up to £5K per week.
  I was responsible for a project worth £1M and line management and supervision of up to 10 staff.

- Avoid vague statements that may sound good but do not provide specific information about what you did, such as "we developed a strategy and my team won the best sales team award". The more specific and clear you are about what you did, the more effective you will come across.

c) Outcome (~15 – 20%)

- Indicate clearly the results of your actions. Was the problem solved? What skills did you gain? Did you meet the targets?

- It is recommended that you choose examples with positive outcomes. However, if your outcome was not successful or if you did not achieve your goal then state what you learnt from the experience. For example; "The project was not successful, however, I have learnt the importance of effective planning and organising such as ...."

"I know I have learnt from my mistakes and have become a more confident and self-assured person as a result"

8) Understand the definition of each competency required

- This will make it easy for you to answer the question following the S.B.O structure.

Communication – ensuring that the message or information delivered is clear and understood.

Team working – working together effectively as a group to meet goals and objectives.

- In addition to knowing the definition you must also know how to use it in your answers. You need to ask yourself more details on how you can demonstrate the definitions in your answers, for example; **"HOW did you ensure that the message/information delivered was clear and understood?" "HOW did you work as a group to meet the goals and objectives?** These are the actions you took to demonstrate effective communication and team working.

- It is important to know the positive behavioural characteristics as mentioned previously for each competency – For example an effective team worker will display characteristics, such as communicating openly with colleagues, sharing information, supporting each other and being a good team player.

- *Now use specific examples where you had to "communicate/share/support/display good team spirit within the team".*

Some useful feedback from Graduate Recruiters

- Candidates use the same examples to answer different questions whether relevant or not.

- Candidates do not distinguish their personal contributions to a group effort and tend to use "we" instead of "I".

- Candidates limit themselves due to lack of preparation, often citing the same experiences time and again, while a range of examples would prove much more impressive.

Pre-Reg Pharmacy – Hospital Interview Questions

A list of pharmacy interview questions but you can use these questions for any other non-pharmacy related job interviews and practice.

<u>Southport/Ormskirk Hospital</u>

- Clinical Governance
- Why this hospital?
- Strengths and weakness
- Future of Pharmacy

Victoria Hospital

- Tell us about yourself?
- What would you say is your biggest weakness?
- Why did you choose this hospital?
- What do you think to the idea of being taught by staff members other than the pharmacist?
- What do you like about university?
- What are your hobbies?
- What will you do on qualification?

Dewsbury Hospital

- Why did you choose pharmacy?
- What do you think hospital pharmacy entails?
- What are your views about prescribing in the future?
- What did you like most about your community placement and what did you find least enjoyable?
- Research question based on application form
- What comes first the patient or the costs?
- NICE and clinical governance – what do you think of them?

Leeds NHS Trust

- How have you prepared for the interview?
- Do you have any preferences for a hospital base out of the hospitals at the Trust i.e. do you have an interest in a certain area in particular? e.g. Transplants, chemotherapy, aseptic production and why?
- What do you see as the role of a Hospital Pharmacist?
- What did you hope that the role of the Pharmacist would be in 10 years time?
- What had you read in a journal e.g. PJ recently which interested you and why?

- They also asked me about extra-curricular activities on my C.V.
- Did I particularly want to work at this hospital and if so why?
- Do you have any previous hospital experience?

Leeds NHS Trust/Leeds Hospital

- Where will you be in 5 years?
- What are your hobbies?
- What does a clinical safety pharmacist do (well something like that!)
- Why Leeds?
- Why are you suitable for this post?
- Anything new you can bring to the team?
- Experiences learnt on placements/vacation placements
- Describe a project done at university/placement

Northallerton Hospital

- What are your strengths?
- What would you say your main weakness was?
- What can you bring to the company? What have you got to offer?
- What do you expect from us? (i.e. the hospital)
- Why did you pick this particular hospital over another one?
- What experience have you got?
- Have you worked in a hospital before? If not, do you know anything about hospital pharmacy? If so what?
- What do you know about any current developments in Pharmacy? i.e. PJ stuff
- What was the last challenging project you took part in? What was your role?

Pinderfields Hospital

- Where do you see yourself in 5 years?
- What influenced you to opt for a career in pharmacy?
- Why did you choose this hospital?

Leeds Teaching Hospital NHS Trust

- Have you ever worked in a Hospital pharmacy? If yes, tell me about your experience and where and what you did.
- What aspects are there to hospital pharmacy? E.g. med info, clinical ward work, aseptics.
- Why do you want to work in hospital pharmacy?
- Why do you want to work for Leeds Hospitals?
- What do you understand by clinical governance?
- What is your opinion on technicians checking and to a certain level clinical checking?
- Have you read about any recent articles in the journal?
- Any questions?

Blackpool Hospital

- Why did you choose Pharmacy?
- Why Blackpool Hospital?
- How are you finding your university course?
- What would be your least favourite area of your course?
- What do you already know about hospital pharmacy?
- Question related to application form (situation relating to overcoming conflict) – How would you feel about dealing with a similar situation in a hospital/What have you learnt from it?/Would you do anything different?
- What are your hobbies and interests?

- You will be working with differently qualified staff (not always the pharmacists) dispensers, nurses etc. How do you feel about that?
- What made you choose the 5 year sandwich course over the 4-year continuous course?

Huddersfield Hospital

- Why Pharmacy?
- Why Huddersfield Hospital?
- Have you read an article in the PJ recently? Why did the article interest you?
- What are the differences between community and hospital pharmacy?
- Have you ever spotted a clinical error whilst on placement?

Nottingham Hospital

- Why Nottingham?
- Where do you see yourself in 3 years time?
- What can Pre-Reg offer the hospital?
- How do you balance your social and educational life?
- What should we look for in a Pre-Reg?
- How has your course prepared you for pharmacy (in the real world)?
- Describe a situation where you have intervened to reduce a risk to a patient.
- What transferable skills have you learnt from university?
- What issues will affect hospital pharmacy in the next few years?
- How would your friends describe you?
- What can you give/offer us?

CHAPTER 8

Managing your money

"Those who don't manage their money will always work for those who do"

One of the biggest challenges I faced at university was managing my finances. Many students get very excited in their first year, the excitement of being independent, living away from home with access to student loans, credit cards, grants and overdraft facilities.

The joy of being able to do what you want, when you want and with who you want sometimes leads to uncontrollable spending. There is always a social event every night, lots of cheap drinks and massive student discounts. The pressures of trying to fit in with the crowd, buy the latest designer wear or fashionable car to impress.

I learnt some hard financial lessons at university. I made many mistakes which taught me valuable lessons which I will share with you in this chapter.

The first lesson that I learnt was, *your bank account determines your performance*. The better you are at managing your money, the more focused you will be on your studies. It is crucial to have a plan to manage your money. Have a plan from the start and don't spend your money randomly.

Learning how to manage your money effectively will not only help you throughout university or college but it is also a skill which will benefit you throughout your professional and personal life.

Financial planning evolves and gets more complicated as you get older and when you complete university. You will have more financial responsibilities, bigger budgets to manage, bigger projects, savings to make for yourself, your family and employers.

However, it is a lot easier managing your money as a student. University is the best opportunity to develop vital money management skills which will benefit you throughout life.

1) BUDGETING

"Spend less than you get"

The simplest and most effective student plan is called a **budget**. A budget is very simple and follows the key principle to financial success *"Spend less than you earn"*.

This is the golden rule which you must memorise. So how does this apply to students when you don't earn yet? This is the biggest mistake I made at university. I thought I couldn't budget until I was earning a full time salary. But budgeting is very important for students too as illustrated over the next pages.

For most of us, this is very challenging and most students spend more than they get and are in debt because we live in a society that encourages us to spend more than we get. A 'buy now and pay later' philosophy. Our standards and living costs are quite high and they make us spend more.

2 Income

Where does most of a student's income come from? There are a few ways but I will focus on the main ones which are; student loans or grants, family support (example; parents/grandparents) and part time jobs.

Use the formula below to work out your student income

student loan or grant + money from family + part time job = Income

This figure should be your reference point. You need to spend less than this figure to manage your money effectively.

Working out your income is quite straight forward. However, your expenditure is a bit more complicated because it is subjective and varies between each student and what they value the most.

How much you spend is determined by your personality, your values and priorities. Because our spending habits are very subjective, they are different for each student. Let me show you a model which can help you work out your student expenditure or expenses.

Needs vs wants

"If you buy things you do not need, soon you will have to sell things you need"

To figure out your expenditure, you must first recognise the difference between things that you *need* versus things that you *want*. Needs are absolute necessities, things which you must have, for example food. Wants are things which you can do without and are not necessities for example; a car.

Your goal is to pay for all your needs first and then spend any extra money on your wants. The challenge for most of us is distinguishing between both. There are many things which we think we need at university which we really don't.

Our expenditures are subjective, but we can agree on a few common needs for example; we need to pay our tuition fees, we need to pay for our accommodation, we need to buy food and we need to buy books.

These are basic needs for every student, but after these needs are met, it becomes subjective because all the other needs are debatable as to whether they are needs or wants based on each students' values and beliefs.

For example, if I asked you, do you need a car at university? Some students may say no and others may say yes. It all depends on whether using this car is an investment, whether it supports your budget or not. For example, if your parents pay for the car, your insurance, tax, repairs, petrol and maintenance, then it is an investment, or if you live far away from campus and cannot get to university via public transport then it's an investment.

But if you were responsible for maintaining the car, you were responsible for paying the tax, the insurance, repairs, petrol, and parking, then it is not a necessity and definitely not an investment. You do not need the car and may be better off using a form of public transport, as this will be more cost effective and will have a positive impact on your budget.

Negative spending associations

You need to be mindful of negative spending habits. Negative habits deplete your budget. You need to become conscious and aware of little habits which negatively impact on your spending.

For example, if every Friday after lectures you routinely meet up with friends at the student union bar, or if during lecture breaks you routinely buy a chocolate bar, a muffin or a coffee from the vending machine, then after a while these small spending habits add up to becoming a major spending expenditure.

Let me expand with a more detailed example. If you have lectures from Monday to Friday and every morning on your way to lectures you routinely buy a Starbucks coffee which costs (£3), then during lecture breaks you buy a drink and a snack from the vending machine for another (£3), followed by a routine lunch in the canteen for £5 and every Friday night you go out for a meal and then a night out with friends and spend £30, that's a total expenditure of more than £4,000 a year.

What would you do if you had that £4000 in your possession all at once? Would you spend it all on coffee, snacks and meals? For most of us the answer would be a resounding no, but if they are done as little negative spending habits associated with other activities, they go unnoticed. You need to become aware of any negative spending associations and break the habits or else it would cost you.

Credit & loans

Student life can be very expensive depending on where you study. Studying in some cities such as London is very expensive. There will be moments when you desire certain things but won't have the money to afford them. This will push you to borrow money, to get now and pay later.

You may obtain the money as a bank loan, credit card, overdraft or loan from a friend or family member. You may have bigger expenses such as buying a car, paying your tuition or even buying a house.

Most students usually do not have the money to pay for these three things upfront and end up borrowing money for them, unless you have wealthy parents or grandparents to pay them off for you.

Let me share with you an important distinction I discovered later in my student life. I didn't know this earlier and I suffered the consequences and I made several regrettable decisions. However, when I learnt this lesson, I became very careful when it came to borrowing money from lenders and organisations.

This is the lesson, *"**Anytime you buy something on credit, you are accepting to pay back more than the item is worth"** and in some cases this agreement could be very detrimental

when you borrow money to pay for something from a lender, all you are saying is 'I am willing to pay more for it than its actual value'.

The best deal you can get as a student is to buy everything up front at its cash value. For example; if a drink costs £5, you pay exactly £5 and get the drink. That's paying at its cash value.
However, if you decide to borrow and then repay in instalments, then you end up paying about £7 pounds in the long term above the original value of the drink.

This extra £2 on the £5 is called *interest*

You need to spend on things that are investments, things that will bring you a good return in the future, things which will *appreciate* over time and not *depreciate.*

This is why the example of the car is very important. Is buying a car an investment? Buying a car in itself is not an investment. Why? Because what happens to the value of a new car once you buy it? From the day you buy it, the value of the car starts to depreciate (decrease). Imagine going to a BMW car dealer and buying a brand new BMW which is worth £40,000. The moment You drive the car out of the garage, the value depreciates and within a couple of months, the value is now about £35,000. It has already depreciated by about £5000 just by you buying it and driving it for a few months.

Now let's look at another example, buying a house. Is buying a house an investment? Yes, it is. Why? Because compared to a car, if you buy a house in a good area and you take good care of it, over time the value of the house *appreciates* (goes up). So you buy a house for £300,000, after a few years, the value of the house goes up to £320,000. The extra 20,000 is called *equity* and it can be turned into cash once you sell your house. It's the extra investment you have made on the house over time. Buying a house in a good housing market is a good investment.

The lesson here **is always borrow money for things that appreciate in value over time and not for things that depreciate.** Borrow money for things which will add value to your life later.

Student loans

Are student loans investments? A university degree typically costs about £9,000 for tuition annually and depending on where you study and also your/family financial circumstances you may get a maintenance loan of up to about £6,000 a year. These are very large figures, roughly about £60,000 at the end of a 4 year degree like pharmacy.

This is a huge debt for anyone finishing university and will have a significant impact on your life after university in terms of your various financial goals after university, but you will still have to repay this loan. This may affect your personal plans such as getting married, buying a house, having kids, putting your children into private schools and travelling.

You can't escape paying back, and the money will be automatically deducted when you start earning above a certain threshold. If you don't pay it back, the financial institutions will do whatever they can to recover the money, deduct from your wages and give you a bad credit score.

So are student loans an investment? Well I already mentioned above that you need to invest in things that will appreciate over time.

When you graduate from university, your earning potential is about *£25,000* a year higher than if you went straight to work after high school. So a high school graduate will make about *£15,000* a year while a university graduate will make about *£40,000* a year on average. That's about a *£25,000* a year difference. If you multiply that over a 40-year work career, that's *£1 million*. A good university degree despite the huge cost in tuition fees, offers you an opportunity to make £1 million pounds more throughout your work career than if you did not attend university.

If you compare the £60,000 of student loan which you borrowed compared to the £1 million pounds which you will earn over the course of your career, then a student loan is a significant investment. Does this make sense?

Don't borrow money for trivial activities, don't borrow to feed your ego, to live a lavish lifestyle, to party all night, to travel and shop excessively or spend on things which don't add any extra value in the long term. Borrow money to invest. Borrow money wisely.

Credit cards and interests

Credit cards are very risky because of the extra interest charges and the interest rates. If you are not careful and if you do not understand fully how credit cards work, you may think they are helpful because you can use them to purchase for things now and then pay later.

But there is a catch, imagine you saw a laptop which you really want on offer for £500, unfortunately you don't have the money to buy it. So you decide to pay for it on your credit card. You buy the laptop and a month later you get your bill to say your balance is £500.

You didn't have this amount at the start of the month, so chances are slim you will have it now. But there is an option to make a minimum payment, fantastic.

You decide to opt for the minimum payment, all you need to pay is £10 each month and that sounds like an amazing agreement to you. That's a great and stress free option isn't it?

So you make a payment of £10 and the credit card company pops the biggest bottle of champagne. This is because you just agreed to pay them more in the long term than if you had made the full £500 payment all at once. The quicker you repay, the less it costs. In fact, if you had paid the full £500 at once, they won't have made any money from you.

If you buy a car for £3,000 at university at an interest rate of 17.9% at 21 years old and you just make minimum credit card payments each month, guess how old you would be before it's cleared? 50 years old. Don't fall into the minimum payment trap, it will lock you in perpetual debt while simultaneously boosting the banks' profits.

The longer you borrow for, the more interest you are charged. You falsely think the companies are helping you by charging you a minimum payment, but the reverse is true. It's in the company's interest to set minimum payments low, so you stay in debt for longer and repay more interest.

This is the credit trap which you must avoid. The aim of the credit companies is to keep you in debt for longer, to make you pay the smallest amount possible over the longest period of time. As your debt decreases, they will also decrease your minimum payments automatically making the debt last longer but the interest payments will increase. It will take you 27 years to pay off the car if you only paid the minimum payment and cost £4,000 in interest. So you will end up paying £7,000 for a car which initially cost £3,000. In the first month you will pay

£71.50 but this decreases monthly down to approximately £6 in about 20 years.

But if you choose to pay a fixed amount £71.50 each month regardless and kept the amount fixed regardless of the new lower minimum payments the companies offer you, then you will clear the debt in just five years and the interest cost will be £1,500, a saving of over £2,400.

Many students make just the minimum repayments because they are either not aware of the financial trap and dangers or because they just can't afford to pay more.

What's the solution? The minimum payment trap is based on you paying minimum payments, the more debt you've repaid, the lower your repayments go. You can overcome this trap by making a fixed repayment based on what you can afford rather than by the decrease the financial companies offer you each month. Also try your best to pay more each month than the minimum repayment.

Credit cards in themselves are not evil if used wisely to invest, but they are one of the single riskiest financial vehicles you can have in your possession. Be extremely careful.

Credit Score

The financial companies always have an eye on your spending habits. They are watching your every move. You may not be aware, but they are. They monitor your activities by giving you a credit score. The higher your score, the better your chances of obtaining loans. One of the biggest mistakes I made at university was, I thought *"what happens at university stays at university"* but this was a big mistake, not with your credit score.

I learnt the hard way. When I graduated from university, my wife (girlfriend at the time) and I saw a lovely house for rent in a beautiful area. We were both so excited and went to visit the property. Everything was perfect and my girlfriend was so ecstatic. It was her dream house. I was doing my pre-reg year and I could afford the rent so I thought there was no problem.

After viewing the house to rent and putting in our joint application to the agency, we received a letter to say our application had been declined. I was shocked, I had a job with enough money to pay the rent. I was told by the agency that the reason the application was declined was because I had a bad credit score from missed payments at university and as a result we could not get the house until I improved my credit score and we lost the offer.

I was devastated, needless to say my wife didn't speak to me for 2 weeks. But this taught me a real lesson. It was an eye opener, that what you do at university does not always stay at university and may catch up with you later in life. How you manage your money at university or college will affect your future. No one taught me this at university.

If you miss scheduled payments, direct debits, standing orders, your credit score decreases and that will stay on your credit report for a while. Protect your credit score, there'll be a point later in your life where it will make a huge difference.

Gross income vs net income

"My problem lies with reconciling my gross habits with my net income"

Be careful with your first pay cheque after university. When you start making money you will get very excited and you will be over the moon because you have just had your first job and you are making good money. When I first qualified as a pharmacist, I was excited. I saw my salary and contract and I became euphoric. I was like a child in a chocolate shop. I wanted to buy everything. I bought a new car, moved into a bigger house, bought expensive furniture, went shopping and booked a few holidays.

I based all my calculations on my gross income rather than my net income. I calculated from my gross salary what I would get monthly and that's what got me very euphoric.

But I was shocked when I received my first pay cheque. I had made all my plans based on my gross income and I was expecting a certain amount at the end of the month.

Yet I was horrified when I got my first pay cheque. I realised I had made all my calculations from my gross income not net income. I had not included my taxes, N.I contributions and the student loan repayments which were a huge junk deducted from my gross salary. I was outraged.

My first pay day which I looked forward to with great anticipation ended up being my greatest nightmare. I was paid on the last day of the month and I was broke the next day.

More money went out than I expected, in fact more went out compared to what came in. It was a disgusting experience and something I won't wish on anyone.

You have two ways to rectify this. You can either earn more money by getting a better paid job or by making some extra income on the side to compensate. Otherwise, you will have to go through the most common option for most students which is to cut back massively on your spending.

I did not need to get a big house, a flashy car, brand new furniture, shopping, and book all those holidays abroad. It was my first real job and I had studied 5 years for this moment. I was excited and got carried away.

But I learnt a lot from this experience. When you get your first job, the contract you will be offered will be a gross salary. Do not make your financial plans from this figure, take away about 30% to get your net figure and use your net figure to make your financial plans.

Pay yourself first (the law of compounding)

"Do not save what is left after spending, but spend what is left after saving"

The law of compounding is one of the most powerful and simple financial laws. I wish I knew this when I started working. Whenever you get your income, you need to pay yourself first before paying anyone else. Take **5-*10%*** out of your student income and put it in your savings. So if you get roughly £1,000 student loan every month and earn £300 monthly from a part time job, then at the end of the month, put £65- £130 directly into your savings account. 5-10% won't really make a significant difference to your lifestyle and you may not even notice it. Live on 90%-95% of your monthly income.

If you start this early enough, as soon as you get your first paid job you will be at an advantage as you will still have several work years ahead of you. This amount of time allows you to save through the law of compounding or the law of 72.

The law requires you to put your money into a savings account where it earns interest, then divide the interest by 72, that means every 7.2 years your money is going to double.

For example; if you finish university and start working at the age of 24 and save £400 a month. If You save this money each month, by the time you retire, you would have saved over £200,000 pounds if that account had an interest rate of about 8%.

This is the law of compounding interest. It requires patience and saving a small amount consistently over many years. It's a get rich slow scheme.

You don't need to save this amount if you can't afford it, the aim is to save whatever you can monthly and build interest on it. The earlier you start doing this even at university, the better.

CHAPTER 9

Happiness and fulfilment

In this chapter, I want to talk about happiness and fulfilment. One of the states we all want to have is a state of happiness. Most of what we do daily consciously or unconsciously are acts to make us happy and fulfilled in some way. Many of us have different ways in which we satisfy our need to be fulfilled.

For some people this is done through positive methods such as helping others, charity, financial, spiritual and career growth.

Others fulfil this need in negative or detrimental ways such as doing drugs, inflicting pain on others, gossiping, eating and drinking excessively or being promiscuous.

The way we choose to satisfy our desire to be happy usually determines our destiny. It determines the actions we take, the social network we have and it drives our lives towards different directions.

There are certain key areas in our lives which determine our happiness. After interviewing so many students, I noticed that there are some key areas which you must focus on if you want to be fulfilled at university. If you are not fulfilled in these areas, then you will be discontent.

Happiness by itself is not a permanent state. It is not a fixed emotion. Our states are constantly changing based on our focus and our physiology at different times. Happiness in my opinion requires constant habits and actions towards attaining it daily.

For example; how do you maintain a happy relationship? Do you just tell your partner I love you once, or spend time with them once a year and that's it? No, you have to do certain actions daily. You have to spend time daily, be caring daily, be affectionate, patient, kind, honest, speak to them daily for them to feel in this state of love and happiness constantly.

The moment we stop some of these habits then our partners, family or friends become unhappy.

No one is happy all the time, we all have moments when we are happy and other moments when we feel down based on what is happening in our lives at that specific time.

Many distinctions have been made between happiness and fulfilment. Fulfilment is usually linked to a greater state of happiness, tranquillity and balance. It's a term more commonly linked to spirituality and a higher purpose.

Many students chase over material things hoping that they'll make them happy. How many times have you heard someone say, if I buy this car or this dress I'll be happy, if I get this job I'll be happy, if I made this amount of money or won the lottery I'll be happy, if I dated this type of boy or girl I'll be the happiest person in the world, if I lost weight and looked like this I'll be ecstatic?

But how many times have you seen people who have all the physical trappings of success but are still unhappy? How many times do you see people or hear of people who seem to have it all, millions of pounds, fame, admiration, career success, all sorts of material wealth, look extremely stunning but are still very unhappy and depressed and in extreme circumstances even commit suicide?

I learnt from an early teacher and mentor that "No Thing" makes us happy. Our happiness is not based on things directly but rather from the feelings we get from them.

For example when you say "if I win the lottery I'll be happy", it is not the money itself that makes you happy but the feelings you ascribe to money such as security, respect, appreciation and ability to contribute.

The same applies if we buy an expensive car like a Lamborghini. It's not the car that makes us happy but the feelings of uniqueness, prestige and attention from others.

Let's focus on the key areas of life which you need to constantly work on to maintain a balance. Taking actions to improve these areas daily will make you more stable, balanced and fulfilled.

When any of these areas in your life are not balanced, then you feel unhappy and stressed. When you speak to people who are usually unhappy or stressed about something, it's usually due to an imbalance in one of these areas.

My life became a lot more balanced and I became more in control of my state and wellbeing the moment I started working on these areas daily. I have made it a habit daily to always take some actions in these areas and as a result I feel a lot happier on a daily basis.

When I ignore or neglect these daily actions in any of these areas then I become stressed and agitated.

These are the key areas of fulfilment;

1) **Finances**

The lack of money or inappropriate management of money is usually one of the greatest sources of stress and unhappiness in our lives. Most of us become unhappy when we have no money, feel broke or poor and not able to do things we enjoy such as shopping, going out with friends, contributing and having that general sense of security.

Many friendships have been destroyed, many families, marriages and important relationships have all been broken due to money related issues.

The first area which you must take full control of to be happy is your finances. You must ensure you manage your money effectively and that you have a positive, not a negative bank balance. You need to take actions daily for example minimising your expenses, spending on your needs not wants, saving and developing good spending habits. Work on clearing your debts and living within your means. Invest in the right activities and do things which help you invest more money.

Manage your money at university effectively, budget and keep a positive bank balance.

Exercise

Write down certain actions you'll take daily to maintain a positive bank balance.

2) Career/education

Most of us spend more time at university than at home. Our course is very important to us. For some students, their degree is the most important or valued area of their life. They spend the majority of their time studying. It's important to have a satisfying and stable course.

One of the common sources of unhappiness among students or sources of stress is course related. When you are not happy at university, not enjoying your course or don't like what you are studying or university life, then you become demotivated.

I have spoken to a number of students who are very unhappy and the main reason is because they don't like their course or degree. As a result, they are less enthusiastic and sometimes feel very confused, indecisive and less passionate about pharmacy.

We spend most of our time at university, and if you don't enjoy your degree, then this means you are spending the majority of your time in a place that you don't like or are not happy with, this means you are in an unhappy state the majority of the time and this puts your life out of balance.

To be truly fulfilled, you need to enjoy your degree. Set goals or daily actions which will enhance your course satisfaction. Read pharmacy related articles, attend pharmacy seminars, join new pharmacy networks, learn new skills.

Exercise: Write down a few actions which you will take daily to enjoy your pharmacy degree more.

3) Relationships

Our relationships are a key area of our lives which is very important for our general wellbeing and happiness at university. Most of the time, I can tell when a friend has had an argument with their partner. They look down and irritated.

Our relationships with our friends, family, loved ones, work colleagues and people around us affect our state. Most of us feel delighted when we spend a lovely day or weekend with family, friends or loved ones.

Having healthy relationships at home and at university is vital and has one of the greatest effects on your happiness. Most students who are truly happy and fulfilled value their relationships with family and friends.

One of the key values I instilled in my staff at work is respect and positive relationships with each other. I have noticed that when there is good communication and mutual understanding between my staff they really enjoy work. No matter how stressful the day is, they are still very happy at work because they feel valued, and respected by each other. They have fun together, tease each other, laugh, support each other and truly care for each other.

Work becomes fun and your colleagues become an extension of your family. I also notice when the staff all get on with each other, there is less absence and greater productivity. It's a great atmosphere and a healthy place to work.

You need to do things daily to improve your relationships if you want to be happy. For example, call your parents or siblings daily to find out how they are and tell them you love them, reconnect with good old friends, go out with family or work colleagues, tell your partner how much you love them, support a work colleague or university colleague with something they are struggling with, something to make their work or life easier.

Exercise: write down things which you'll do daily to make sure you improve relationships with family, friends and work colleagues.

4) Health & wellbeing

We've all heard the phrase *'your health is your wealth'*. Your happiness is affected by your health. How do you feel when you are sick or physically unwell? Do you feel excited, energetic and ready to make a difference? No, you feel weak, in pain, miserable and unhappy.

So to be truly happy and fulfilled we must value our health and take action daily to ensure we are fit and healthy. This puts us in a positive state of mind and body. We feel more energetic, more revitalised and have a general and positive outlook.

When most of us are unwell, we are very irritable, we are very unhappy and have a negative outlook. Being a pharmacist and dealing with many patients daily, I come across many people who are very unhappy due to their health. Their poor health prevents them from doing the things they really want to do, things which will allow them to experience the feelings of being content that they desire and deserve.

It is important therefore that we focus daily on performing and maintaining healthy habits which will contribute positively to our wellbeing and happiness. The moment we ignore our health, ignore exercising or eating healthily we create a perfect environment for poor health and eventually end up developing an illness or disease which robs us of the happiness, physical and mental balance that we deserve.

Doing certain acts daily like eating healthy and exercising is important to maintaining good health and happiness.

Exercise: Write a number of healthy things you'll do......

In addition, as mentioned in previous chapters, always continue to grow in all areas of your life, keep learning and keep improving. Finally, contribute in whatever way you can, give back to your family, friends and society at large. Focusing on these six keys will keep you to be happy and fulfilled.

CHAPTER 10

7 principles to succeed on exam day

In this chapter, I will share with you 7 principles to pass your exam. These are very important actions which you must do or avoid on the day of your exam to excel.

Your performance on the day of the exam will be based on your state. You can't learn much at this stage and your main focus should be to build your confidence and stay positive. Avoid any form of negative talk or anything which will make you anxious or put you in a disempowered state.

Here are the 7 principles

1 Focus on what you want

This principle is very important because when it comes close to exam day, whatever you focus on, you experience. The challenge is most of us focus on what we don't want before an exam as oppose to what we want. How many times do you hear students say I will fail? The exam will be hard? I have not read this or that topic? I have not read anything? I am so scared of this exam?

To be relaxed and successful on the day of the exam you need to focus on what you want. Focus on being motivated, focus on being positive, focus on what you have read, focus on passing, focus on being relaxed. This is the state you need to be in to be resourceful and to pass your exam.

2 Focus on what you get right

Focus on what you get right not what you get wrong. Generally, when we go into exams, we focus on the questions we get wrong and not on those which we get right. What do most students think about when they come out of exams? It's mostly what they got wrong? Some students write down their answers during the exams and discuss them later outside, how many times have you seen this?

You need to focus on what you got right because any form of negativity will affect your state, your mood and your performance in other exams. I do many coaching sessions with pharmacy students before their exams and most of the students tell me they are very stressed. I asked them why? They say, "I did a past paper and I got everything wrong" when I ask them "everything?" then they say I got 5, 6, 7 or 8 questions wrong. Then I ask, "how many did you get right?" and they say about 40 or 50. They change their state and immediately become more positive the moment they start focusing on what they got right rather than what they got wrong and that helps them do better.

When you go into your exam, always focus on the questions you are getting right and you will feel very positive and increase your chances of succeeding

3. You can't learn everything

Many students get stressed and anxious before exams because they are trying to cover every single topic and know everything before an exam. But you can't learn everything. Can you remember an exam which you passed but did not cover every single topic before the exam? Confidence before an exam comes from being confident with what you know. Focus on perfecting what you already know on the day of the exam and don't try learning new things.

Trying to learn new things on the day of the exam will make you less confident. It's what I call 'perfection paralysis', where you focus on trying to learn everything and be perfect that you get paralysed and your brain freezes. You become too stressed and lose your confidence. If you keep focusing on what you don't know, you won't be confident about how much you already know.

4.See things as they are

See things as they are and not worse than they are. What most of us do before exams is we generalise and blow things up in our minds. I realised this pattern with many of the students I coach. For example, if they think they failed 5 questions in a 20 question exam, they say 'I failed everything'.

These sort of generalisations make us see things worse than they are and affect our performance negatively. Give an honest and positive view and don't exaggerate or generalise any negative perceptions. If you have to improve or learn 3 more topics, say you have to learn 3 more topics, not you have to learn everything. This realistic view will empower you and motivate you to succeed. Remember what we focus on we experience, what you say to yourself you experience, so be very careful about the things you say to yourself on the exam day or few days leading to the exam. Say positive things to yourself and see your situation exactly as it is and not worse than it is.

5. Believe first

Most students only believe they can pass an exam only when they have actually seen the exam. One of the pharmacy students I coached before an exam told me she can't see herself passing the exam until she actually passes the exam.

That's the problem because you need to believe before you can achieve. To succeed you must first visualise yourself passing the exam. You believe first before you see. Some students will only be confident the moment they see the exam paper. If you need to see things first before you believe, then you rub yourself of a special force within you that can give you the confidence you need before entering an examination room.

We've all heard of the placebo effect where patients are given a dummy pill or empty capsule and told it's a real pill. They get better even though they took an empty capsule. The reason is because they believed they were taking a real pill and their belief transformed their bodies to produce the result. This is the power of belief. If you believe you will succeed before you do the exam, you will transform your body and mind to produce that result. Have you passed other exams in the past? If the answer is yes, then use this as evidence that you will pass again in the future

6. Embrace your fear, don't fight it

Most of us get nervous before an exam because we are afraid we may not pass or the exam may be difficult. We have learned to deal with fear by trying to fight it. We say to ourselves 'I don't want to be nervous' 'I don't want to fail' 'I don't want to be stressed' and we try to fight our fear.

Stress is an emotion and it is there to help you. learn to use your fear rather than let it use you. It is just a signal to alert you to get ready for the unknown. I coached a student who always felt very anxious before every exam but the moment she sat down and started the exam, the fear went away and she always performed well. I showed her how to use her fear to help her and not fight against it.

Next time you feel anxious, realise its normal and this fear is your friend trying to remind you to be prepared. Thank your fear for the message, feel the fear and go on and do the exam. There'll always be a form of stress and anxiety before an exam, everyone experiences it even first class students do. The only difference is they learn how to use it rather than let it use them. Don't fight it, embrace it. Feel the fear and do it anyway.

7 Stay Internal

Many things will happen on the day of the exam to distract you. You will see, hear and feel things that may affect your state, that may make you feel you are not prepared or may fail

For example, you may see certain students reading certain topics outside the examination hall which you did not read, or hear certain students discussing certain subjects on you did not cover. Sometimes some students may finish the exam early and make it feel easy. Others will gather in groups to discuss some of the answers after an exam.

All these distractions are external triggers which you must avoid. Stay internal on yourself. Focus on staying positive and distance yourself from these distractions. They'll make you doubt yourself, become nervous and potentially fail. Stay internal.

Conclusion

I will like to conclude by thanking you for reading this book. Thank you for taking action to learn important skills, techniques and philosophies to improve yourself.

Not only are you adding more value to your life, but by buying this book, you are also contributing to improving the lives of many less privileged children. A percentage of all my book sales go to charity to support, empower and give less privileged kids an education and hope. My goal is to help as many less privileged children as possible and see them succeed. This is my goal and thank you very much for supporting this project.

I hope you have learned some valuable tools, information and techniques in this book. There are no results without action. Make a commitment now to take action and achieve your goals. You are special and you have all the skills within you to turn your goals into reality. Share this knowledge with others and be a force for good to the world and always remember the key to living is giving.

STAY STRONG

Follow me on facebook : marvinmunzu

Twitter: @marvinmunzu

Website: www.marvinmunzu.com